Lean Project Management:
Eight Principles for Success

Lawrence P. Leach, PMP

© Advanced Projects, Inc. 2005

5239 South Pegasus Way

Boise, Idaho 83716

www.Advanced-projects.com

Contents

i

iii

It is important that an aim never be defined in terms of activity or methods. It must always relate directly to how life is better for everyone... The aim of the system must be clear to everyone in the system.

W. Edwards Deming (1900 - 1993)

PRINCIPLE ONE: PROJECT SYSTEM

Successful project delivery requires leading the system, comprised of people, process, and product. You must define an effective system for your environment and projects. Lean thinking enhances conventional project delivery systems in the areas of portfolio and individual project planning, execution, and control to eliminate waste and deliver successful project results *"in half the time, all the time"*.

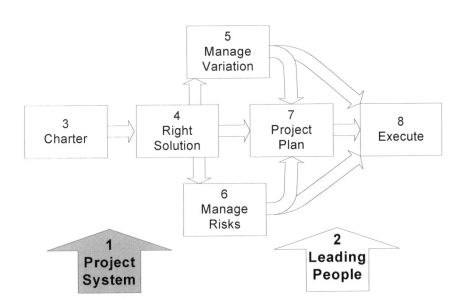

The figure on the previous page illustrates that the project system underlies all of the Principles for Lean Project Management success. All eight principles relate to each other through the project system. While the figure shows a flow for principles three through eight, relationships connect all of the entities in both directions.

Project planning and execution comprise a system, which I call the project delivery system. Some people are intimidated by *system thinking*, likening it to rocket science. The Theory of Constraints (TOC), an approach I have used to develop LPM, asserts that system thinking can and should be simple. This chapter will address the key elements needed to design your Lean project delivery system, with special emphasis on the contributions of Critical Chain Project Management (CCPM) to that system.

People interact with and design systems all the time, often without thinking about it that way. I defined *Critical Chain Project Management* (Leach, 2004) as the synthesis of several systems, including conventional project management, the Theory of Constraints (TOC), and Total Quality Management (TQM, now frequently called Six Sigma). The Lean system continues this synergy to include Lean manufacturing principles, beginning with focusing on eliminating waste.

Project delivery systems deploy people to use processes to create a result: a product or service. As with all systems, the *relationships* between the entities over time determine the results. The relationships in a project delivery system, including most importantly the people, matter more than the entities themselves. For example, how you develop your plan determines how people will perform the work. The way people perform the work influences how you can measure and control it.

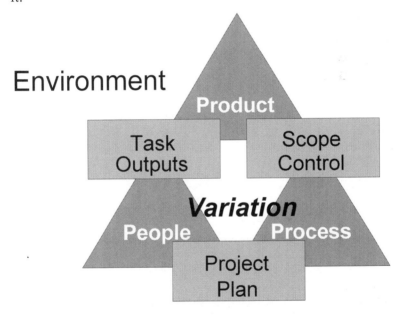

Figure 1-1: A view of the project system as the intersection of People, Process, and the Product the project will produce.

Figure 1-1 depicts a project system comprised of people, process, and the product that the project will produce. The project system functions within the environment of many other systems; some larger; some smaller. Defining a system is always somewhat arbitrary because all things relate to some degree. The figure also shows variation as the central part of the system. TOC and Six Sigma focus on variation, but

3

conventional project management often considers it as a minor point, or part of risk management. The figure illustrates a few of the relationships between the entities shown. There are many more.

Some relate project planning and execution to team sports. It often makes a fair comparison. In the Olympics, well-trained amateur teams frequently triumph over groupings of the world's best individual performers. It is the same with projects.

Dr. W. Edwards Deming, the world famous quality guru, liked to list several things that he felt most management tried to use to improve their system:

- Automation
- New machinery
- Gadgets
- Computers
- Hard work
- Best efforts

After making the list, he would announce in his memorable style, "All wrong!"

Instead, Deming emphasized that, *"Management of a system requires knowledge of the **inter-relationships** between all the sub-processes within the system and everybody that works in it"*. I developed LPM to focus on and exploit knowledge of the whole project delivery system. This involves much more than scheduling, the focus of critical chain. Of course, the actual project delivery system differs between organizations, and even between projects within the same organization. Consequently, it is up to you to mate the typical robust behaviors and specific needs typical of any project system, including all of your project stakeholders.

Begin With the End in Mind: The PMO?

Many companies have moved to establish Program or Project Management Offices (PMOs). The responsibility assigned to PMOs varies substantially, but a common thread is that the PMO defines the project delivery processes, and thus the project delivery system. Defining the project management processes and system are very good things. PMOs usually also have some degree of responsibility for training to the system, which is also a good thing. Beyond that, approaches to PMOs vary significantly, from full authority for project management, including being the organization home for all project managers, to only having the two functions described above in this paragraph. You might consider a long-range view right from the beginning when you consider how to design your PMO. You do not need to start with the final configuration.

I do not believe that there is a single right answer for how to configure *your* PMO at this point in your company's project delivery maturity. I do however believe that there is an ultimate answer, with a variety of very successful project management companies, including the Worlds largest construction firms. The most successful do not have a PMO as described above or in the literature, because project management is the only way they do business. It is not in addition to their management process, it *is* their management process. For example, one ISO 9001 certified company used ISO 9001 to define the system for how they do projects. All of their training focused on project management, and so forth. Anything less than full integration of the project delivery system into the management system is probably some kind of band-aid. Thus, although I have set up and operated PMOs for companies in the early stages of implementing successful project delivery, in my opinion the ultimate PMO is no PMO at all. The ultimate PMO is just *"the way we do business around here."*

The eight principles approach to the project system, fully integrates CCPM into LPM. Since the critical chain part of

CCPM plays its largest role late in the project planning phase and during execution, and because CCPM supercharges the project system, I describe it along with the other elements of the first principle.

LPM continues the sport team analogy by relating projects to a relay race. The goal is to win the race, which requires moving the baton across the goal line as soon as possible. The baton passes from racer to racer. Relay races often go to those who are best at passing on the baton from racer to racer, over those with the fastest individual runners on their team. U.S. "dream teams" at the Olympics, arguably comprising the best individual talent in the sport, often lose to teams from countries where the sport is an amateur affair. The reason is that the latter have practiced functioning as a team: they have perfected their roles and hand-offs, even though their individual skills may be lacking. If a relay race team has to rework anything (e.g. pick up a dropped baton), they will not win the race. Please think about applying the analogy to your projects.

The Basics Count: PM101

The Project Management Institute's (PMI) *Guide to The Project Management Body of Knowledge* (PMBOK™ Guide) notes, on the first page, *"the project management team is responsible for determining what is appropriate for any given project"*. The reason is that all projects are by definition unique, and that most of the time the project team is new or different as well. Thus, what worked on project x with team y at time x in place w most likely differs from what you need. Understanding the basics enables you to tailor processes to your project and your team. So please do not take anything from here on to mean *"you have to do this."* It is all for your knowledge and skill building. How and when you use it is up to you.

PMI defines a project (p. 5) as *"A temporary endeavor to create a unique product, service, or result"*. That covers a lot

6

of territory, and is one of the reasons that considerable misunderstanding exists about the meaning of projects in a professional sense. Within that definition, your pub-crawl this evening is certainly a project. For our purposes, a project is something with a business purpose, a customer beyond the person(s) performing the work, usually involving a team of people, and extending beyond a week. It is something that requires some degree of planning to be successful. Thus, cleaning your dog after an encounter with a skunk might be *a real project* in the conventional use of the word, but that is not what we have in mind here.

PMI also defines programs and portfolios of projects. A program is a group of projects to achieve some common goal. For example, you may develop a program for a particular automobile design, and have projects to initially design and test it, to build the manufacturing lines to manufacture it, to put in place the supply chain to maintain it, and to modify it over time. A portfolio is a group of Programs or Projects, at a still higher level. For example, a portfolio might be a group of automobiles built on the same frame and sharing parts, or a category such as SUVs. Businesses may not have a program level, but usually have more than one project, thus by definition have a portfolio. The PMBOK® Guide does not really address portfolio management, and we will only address it from the perspective of LPM.

To accomplish projects, PMI addresses processes and knowledge areas. They group the processes in accordance with the general flow for a single project:

1. Initiating.
2. Planning.
3. Execution.
4. Closing.
5. Monitoring and controlling.

7

The groups overlap, and the last group applies to all of the processes. PMI defines the process groups in terms of the inputs and outputs.

One can model any system as a set of linked processes. Every process has suppliers that provide inputs, and outputs that go to customers. Some people call this the **SIPOC** model, for supplier, input, process, output, and customer. For most of the processes in a business, the next operation in the business is the customer. When you link these processes together to get from external suppliers to external customers, you have a value chain for the business system. You can view projects the same way: each task in a project is a process. It requires inputs or completed predecessors, and it creates outputs that go to successor tasks in the project, the sum total of which create the project result.

Figure 1-2 illustrates the nine knowledge areas that PMI has defined for projects. The figure highlights those areas most affected by LPM (Leach, 2004, p. 25). This text covers most of the areas to some degree, but focuses on the areas that relate to LPM.

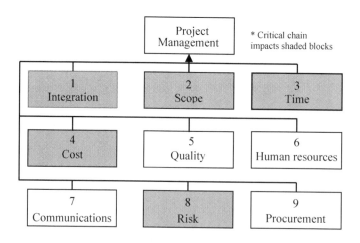

Figure 1-2: PMI defines project management in terms of nine knowledge areas.

LPM is about simplifying project leadership to satisfy your stakeholders in the shortest amount of time, while minimizing stress on project participants and waste. A project leader has to consider a number of elements. The trick is balancing the elements, and deciding when and where to focus.

The latest version of the PMBOK™ Guide includes detailed process flow diagrams for the entire project planning and delivery process. Figure 1-3 is a simplified version that I have used to plan and manage a Project Management Office (PMO). Although at this level, it does not show all of the inputs and outputs, nor the suppliers and customers for each process block, it does provide a snapshot of the overall process.

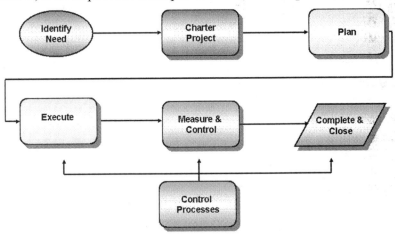

Figure 1-3: The overall project delivery process.

Anderson (2004, pp. 277-300) discusses the relationship of software development characteristics, development methodologies, and organizational maturity as they relate to the type of software product. I feel that his perspective and discussion relates to many project fields. He suggests that the project planning and execution approach that will work best is a function of the characteristics of both the product and the production process.

The approach you should use to manage the design and construction of a bridge differs in many respects from the approach you need to discover and develop a drug or design and deploy a social system. The approach to develop drugs in one company culture may not work at all in another company. Thus, although I believe that at a high enough level Figure 1-3 always applies, the implementation processes to carry it out will vary from organization to organization, and possibly from project to project. One of Stephen Covey's principles from the 8th Habit, *seek first to understand,* applies to the design of your project delivery system (Covey, 2004). The principles of TOC and LPM addressed below seem to work in most project environments, suggesting that they are at a level equivalent to Figure 1-3.

LPM Principles and the Theory of Constraints

Critical Chain Project Management (Leach, 2004) brings together the principles of the Theory of Constraints (TOC), Goldratt's critical chain (Goldratt, 1997), and the PMBOK™. The first TOC principle states that a constraint limits the output of any system. Some prefer this simple statement of the *theory of constraints.* The TOC International Certification Organization (TOC/ICO) poses a more thorough definition:

> *A holistic management philosophy developed by Dr. Eliyahu M. Goldratt that is based on the principle that complex systems exhibit inherent simplicity, i.e., even a very complex system made up of thousands of people and pieces of equipment can have any given time only a very, very small number of variables – perhaps only one (know as a constraint) – that actually limits the ability to generate more of the system's goal.*

I subscribe to most of that definition, although am skeptical about the word "holistic", as effective LPM requires much more than TOC. TOC principles include focusing on the goal, working to maximize throughput in business systems, and deploying five focusing steps to improve systems; the first of which is to identify the constraint to achieving more of the system goal.

Following these principles, and understanding that projects are comprised of interdependent tasks, each of which experiences variation in task performance duration, LPM makes three radical assertions about project management:

- ❏ You do not have to finish each task on time to finish a project on time.

- ❏ Starting a project sooner does not mean it will finish sooner.

- ❏ Adding buffers reduces project duration and cost.

The following sections describe how LPM accomplishes these seeming paradoxes for a single project and in a multi-project system.

A principle that underlies LPM is the principle that *any project worth doing is worth doing fast*. (It is also worth doing right the first time, and I believe that quality and speed are complementary, but that is another story.) The business reason is simple. Most projects do not begin to deliver a return on investment until after project completion. The investment in a project (at least in theory) should be nearly the same, regardless of how long the project takes. Most will agree that a project that takes longer to complete will cost a little more. However, let us put that aside for the moment, as it would only help the point I want you to think about in this case. I think you will also agree that most project results have an effective end of life: a time at which they will no longer continue to deliver a return for their original intent; at least not without another major upgrade project. Reasons include wear-out, obsolescence, or replacement by a superior competitive product, which may be from another project you do.

Table 1-1 compares executing the same project in two years vs. four years. In both cases, the total investment of $4 million produces an annual cash flow of $2 million. Assume that the project result (perhaps a new product) will be obsolete at the end of eight years. You can see that doing the project in half the time improves the return on investment by 50%.

Table 1-1: Any project worth doing is worth doing fast. (*Dollars in thousands.*)

Case	Item	Total	Year							
			1	2	3	4	5	6	7	8
	Investment	$4,000	$2,000	$2,000						
Fast	Return	$12,000			$2,000	$2,000	$2,000	$2,000	$2,000	$2,000
	ROI	3								

Case	Item	Total	1	2	3	4	5	6	7	8
	Investment	$4,000	$1,000	$1,000	$1,000	$1,000				
Slow	Return	$8,000					$2,000	$2,000	$2,000	$2,000
	ROI	2								

Now consider deploying resources (money, people, etc.) to do multiple projects. Would you do better to start all projects at the same time, spreading out your resources, or concentrating your resources on the projects sequentially, so you get each project done in the quickest possible time from when you start it?

Consider table 1-1 again, and assume you have the resources to do the fast project as shown. That means you would start revenue flow (return) on it after two years. Then, you would start the second project in year three and finish it at the end of the fourth year, bringing the total revenue to $4 million at the start of year five.

If you started both projects at once, with your resources split between them, they would both follow the slow project time scale. No revenue would start until year five. Thus, you would forever lose the $ 4 million in revenue you could have had from the first project during years three and four. You will see how LPM implements this principle below.

Information Technology (IT) projects demonstrate notoriously poor performance to the normal project metrics of scope, schedule, and cost. Partly in reaction to this, a host of project delivery approaches have been proposed in recent years to overcome perceived limitations in conventional project leadership. They go by a number of names and acronyms, often categorized as *light* or *agile* approaches. The fundamental principle these techniques seem to operate on is to generate usable product as soon as possible, and improve on that product over time. That approach aligns well with the argument above, considering that returns start with the first usable product. In essence, they are breaking down a large project (which I would label a program) into a series of smaller projects. Some carry it so far as to drive to produce a deliverable every two weeks or month. I suppose in the limit one could approach continuous deliverables, and thus maximize the flow of throughput.

Although the agile approaches provide great ideas for team leadership, a number of them do not deviate from available conventional project management as much as proponents suggest. They do however, promise improvement from mis-application of conventional process. The most common mistake people make with the PMBOK™ Guide is to treat it as a prescription of all the things you have to do for any project or project system. That is like blaming the restaurant for your tummy ache because you tried to eat everything on their menu.

The PMBOK™ has described spiral development processes and rolling-wave planning (or, *progressive elaboration*) from the beginning. Spiral development includes rapid prototyping and deployment approaches, which R&D project managers have used for a long time. Rolling-wave planning involves planning in detail only so far into the future as you know the details. I learned to apply rolling-wave planning to R&D projects in the mid 1970s, and have successfully managed a large number of R&D projects, including IT projects, with the rolling-wave approach. The program to put a man on the moon by the end of the 1960s was an excellent example of rolling-wave planning applied to a very large and uncertain program. The agile IT project techniques do push the time window shorter, which seems appropriate for many IT projects, where the technology continues to evolve at high speed, and incremental functionality is possible. Anderson (2004) demonstrates how to use LPM with agile IT projects. I consider the light or agile techniques as completely aligned to the principle that *any project worth doing is worth doing fast!*

Lean Principles

Lean manufacturing approaches focus on eliminating waste with five key principles:

1. Specify value.
2. Identify the value stream.
3. Flow.
4. Pull.
5. Perfection.

All of these principles synergize well with CCPM. The link to value ties to TOC's focus on the Goal, and Six Sigma's focus on the customer. Identifying the value stream for projects is the project delivery system. Focus on flow relates especially well to the TOC/CCPM multi-project approach, which seeks to maximize the flow of projects through the constraint. For single projects, the critical chain and buffer management implement pull, while for multiple project systems the drum schedule and capacity constraint buffer implement pull.

Many consider Taiichi Ohno, developer of the Toyota Production System, as the father of Lean manufacturing. Ohno (1988) describes a thirty-year process of designing and deploying the elements of what most consider the foundation of Lean.

In one part of his book he states, *"The primary objective of the Toyota production system was to produce many models in small quantities"* (p. 2). He also states (p. xii) that *"The most important objective of the Toyota system has been to increase the production efficiency by consistently and thoroughly eliminating waste."* Ohno put substantial focus on understanding the flow of work, and introduced the relay racer and sports analogies that I use here. The relay racer has become a standard of the CCPM approach to multi-project flow.

Womack and Jones (1996) define eight types of waste (one more than Ohno), called *Muda* in Japanese. They are:

1. Defects in products (i.e. rework).

2. Overproduction of items no one wants.

3. Inventory waiting to be processed.

4. Unneeded processing.

5. Unnecessary movement of people.

6. Unnecessary transport of goods.

7. People waiting for input to work on.

8. Design of goods and services that do not satisfy customer needs.

This book will not address all of the waste types (e.g. item 1) individually, as they easily demand books on their own. The design of LPM considers the relationships to the processes and process steps necessary to reduce all of the types of waste, and you should also do so as you design and deploy your project delivery system.

Cusumano and Nobeoka (1998) seek to move Lean ideas to certain elements of multiple project systems in *Thinking Beyond Lean*. They put attention on "conscious planned efforts to link a set of projects *strategically*, through product portfolio planning, *technologically* through the design of common core components, and *organizationally* through overlapping the responsibilities and work of project managers and individual engineers." This text complements their directions with a focus on multi-project flow.

Management theories overlap as well as complement each other, and in those cases where the overlap seems to conflict, a return to the principles of each can show you the way to resolve the apparent conflict. The TOC perspective is that these conflicts must not be real because all seek the same goal. From my perspective, those that attempt to sell you on the idea that their view is the only one are akin to the six blind men feeling the elephant...they have just grabbed on to different parts of the animal. I do not want you to grab on to my part of the elephant...but I will provide you some input to interpret your part, perhaps in a more useful way.

Single Project LPM Plan

LPM develops a *critical chain*, rather than a critical path, as the primary focus of the project. The approach works to eliminate waste types two, three, and seven above. The critical chain includes BOTH logical (that is, necessary technical task sequence, such as you have to build the first floor before you can build the second) and resource dependence (that is, who is going to do the work). LPM establishes the *critical chain* after removing resource contentions, rather than before considering the resource limitations. The *critical chain* remains unchanged for the entire duration of the project, and is the primary **focus** of the project manager.

Consider the project illustrated by the figure 1-4 Gantt chart. The Gantt chart, named after its creator Henry Gantt, is the most common way to show project schedules. It shows each project task as a bar, with the length of the task bar representing the time estimated for the task. This Gantt chart shows task relationships; i.e. an output from one task becomes the necessary input to another task, defining the task sequence

16

or *relationship*. The figure illustrates the critical path (dark bars): the longest path through the project.

	WBS	Task Name	Low Risk Duration	Gantt Chart
1	1.0	Component 1	30 days	
2	1.1	Design Component 1	10 days	Larry
3	1.2	Build Component 1	10 days	Bill
4	1.3	Test Componenet 1	10 days	Sally
5	2	Component 2	24 days	
6	2.1	Design Component 2	8 days	Larry
7	2.2	Build Component 2	8 days	Bill
8	2.3	Test Componenet 2	8 days	Sally
9	3	Component 3	18 days	
10	3.1	Design Component 3	6 days	Larry
11	3.2	Build Component 3	6 days	Bill
12	3.3	Test Componenet 3	6 days	Sally
13	4	Integration	20 days	
14	4.1	Integrate Componenets	10 days	Jeff
15	4.2	Test Integrated Unit	10 days	Sally
16	5	Project Complete	0 days	3/25

Timeline headers: Jan '05 (2, 9, 16, 23, 30), Feb '05 (6, 13, 20, 27), Mar '05 (6, 13, 20, 27), Apr '05 (3, 10). Critical Path callout box.

Figure 1-4: An example critical path project

The Figure 1-4 project could be a project to design a prototype of some product that involves software and hardware. Given that each task estimate assumes each resource working 100% of their time on the task, how likely is it that project will finish on time? Most people quickly recognize that it is unlikely because the plan calls for several resources to do two or three tasks at the same time. Doing so will stretch out those tasks, by at least a factor of two or three. Thus, it is unlikely the project would complete as scheduled. This is not news to the world of project management, and numerous approaches to resource leveling can resolve this problem. Figure 1-5 illustrates the same project after resource leveling, i.e. adjusting task scheduled dates to make the resource *need* less than or equal to the resource *supply*, in this case one of each person. Note that the project due date moves to the right.

17

Although the resource-leveling capability exists in most project software, few project managers use it. My informal surveys at the PMI Seminars I give (a large portion of the attendees whom are certified Project Management Professionals) indicate that only about 5% of project managers resource level. My review of customer project plans indicates more severe planning problems in a large majority of cases; often using scheduling tools to draw Gantt chart pictures with no resource loading or task relationships, much less resource leveling.

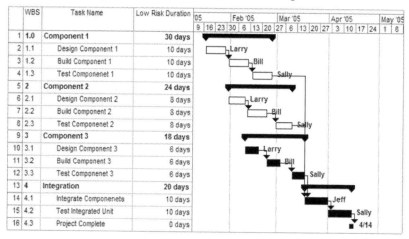

Figure 1-5: The resource leveled critical path project.

Examine figure 1-5 carefully. Notice what happened to the critical path after resource leveling. Every path has a gap in it or before it starts, representing float. The software does not specify the algorithm used to select the particular tasks as critical, and I know that other software (including other versions of the software used) makes different choices. Since, resource leveling often causes all paths to show float, what should the software do?

Identifying the critical chain resolves this conflict. The critical chain is *the longest path through the network after resource leveling*. The critical chain has no float or slack when identified.

18

The critical chain usually differs from the critical path, as it can jump the task logic network. Figure 1-6 illustrates the critical chain for the figure 1-4 task network, comprising tasks 1.1, 1.2, 1.3, 2.3, 3.3, 4.1, and 4.2. Later steps in creating the complete critical chain network may introduce apparent float or slack into the network.

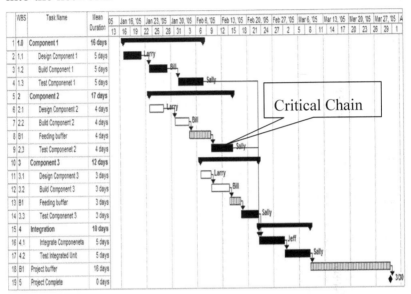

Figure 1-6: Identifying the constraint to a single project: the critical chain, and adding buffers.

Note that the completion date of the critical chain schedule (Figure 1-6) is about the same as the critical path schedule, despite the large project buffer. This illustrates the effect of reducing activity duration to '50/50' duration, and addition of buffers.

The reason for reducing task duration is that all work exhibits variation. If you recorded the times it took you to do the same thing repeatedly (e.g. driving to work), you would find that it varies; usually quite a lot. If you want a project to complete on time, and you do not use buffers, you have to estimate each task at the longest time it could take.

Since all the tasks vary, it is better to estimate each task at its average time, and relocate that extra time from each task to a buffer at the end of the chain of tasks. It requires less total time in a buffer at the end of chain tasks than it does to protect each task because under-runs on some tasks will take care of some of the over-runs on other tasks in the chain. With critical chain plans, you should expect completion before the end of the project buffer, and half the time before the start of the project buffer.

The entities labeled Feeding Buffer in figure 1-6 (tasks 8 and 13) help ensure that both the inputs and the resources are available to start critical chain tasks. *Merging* in a project network means a task requires input from more than one predecessor. In those cases, the successor task cannot start until both of the predecessor tasks complete. This merging synchronization problem delays many projects.

LPM solves the merging problem, and the early-start, late-finish dilemma (i.e. which way to schedule?) with Feeding Buffers (FB). Inserting FBs where each activity chain feeds the critical chain (including the entry to the Project Buffer) helps to immunize the critical chain from delay in these feeding paths. Late starting the feeding chains against these buffers, as allowed by resource leveling, resolves the early/late start question.

Consider an activity on the critical chain that requires inputs from three tasks; one of which is the immediate predecessor on the critical chain, and the other two on parallel network paths. If the tasks estimates assume a 50/50 chance of completing each task within the duration estimate, the chance of having all three is only 1/8 (probabilities multiply). The latest of the three tasks will determine the start time of the common successor task. The feeding buffers add extra time to the non-critical chain paths, moving the predecessors earlier in time, so that the chance of having each of those feeder chain inputs is very high.

This increases the chance of having all three predecessors, and thus the start of the successor task, back up to near 50/50.

Project schedules require determining when to start non-critical chains of tasks. They can start as early as possible (the usual default), called early start, or as late as possible without delaying the critical path or chain, called late start. Early start sometimes helps avoid task synchronization problems. Disadvantages of early start include requiring many paths to start at the beginning of project, when the team is still forming, and causing project cash flow to be higher at the beginning of a project than necessary.

The feeding buffers (combined with the activity dependent schedule created while establishing the critical chain) allows starting activities as late as possible, while protecting the overall project, because the feeding buffers add enough time to ensure the feeding chains are complete when needed (to a high probability). The scheduled start of the feeding chains will be later than early-start times, giving the project the maximum **focus** and cash flow advantages from starting later. Compare the start times of tasks 2.1 and 3.1 in figure 1-4 to their start times in figure 1-6 to see this effect.

Linking Measurement and Control to the Plan

LPM uses buffer management during project execution to answer two primary questions:

1. For project and task managers: "Which task do I work on next?"

2. For the project manager, "When do I take actions to accelerate the project?

Tracking LPM projects requires identifying when tasks start and finish, and obtaining estimates on the remaining duration for tasks in work. LPM uses remaining duration instead of percent complete because some people tend to over-estimate

21

the percent complete. When called upon to look forward and consider the work remaining to complete a task, people tend to make estimates that are more accurate. Remaining duration is also the actual number needed to estimate project completion, and estimating it directly avoids the assumptions necessary to convert a percent complete estimate to a remaining duration estimate.

LPM project tracking then uses the estimates of remaining duration for incomplete tasks to calculate the impact of the task status, including the absorption of variation by feeding buffers, to determine how much of the project buffer has been used. Task managers place priority on the tasks that cause the greatest amount of project buffer penetration. Using task priority this way enables resources to focus on one project task at a time, thereby completing it in the minimum possible time. Tasks do not have due dates. This helps avoid having Parkinson's Law (task durations extend to use available time) or Student Syndrome (waiting to start a task until the due date is urgent) cause late task delivery. The ability to update remaining duration after tasks start also encourages using mean task duration estimates.

The mechanism to complete projects as soon as possible answers two different questions. The answer to the first question, "Which project task should I work on next?" addresses the task and resource manager's need to enable relay racer like task performance, avoiding bad multitasking. The answer to the second question, "When should we take action to recover schedule?" helps the project team decide when to take action to recover buffer used up at too high a rate.

Figure 1-7 illustrates a task manager view into a LPM project that is underway. The tasks are color coded in the task number box on the left (not visible in the graphic) to highlight the priority of the task. Red tasks get the highest priority, as they are on a path that is causing significant project buffer use. The Concerto software used to generate the screen shot is a leading multi-project LPM software that directly provides the task level priority for the multi-project environment.

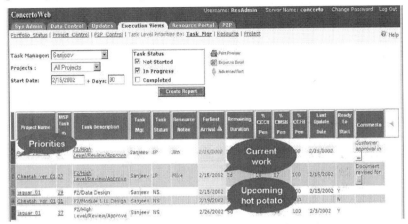

Figure 1-7: Critical chain software updates tasks using remaining duration, prioritizing tasks for work. (Used by permission from Realization, Inc.)

Task level priority does not necessarily match project priority. For a given resource or task manager, a task on a lower priority project may require work more urgently than a task on a higher priority project. The dynamics of an individual project may require that non-critical chain tasks have higher priority than critical chain tasks. These conditions happen when predecessor tasks have caused delays threatening the project buffer more for the lower priority project or non-critical chain.

The amount of project buffer penetration also answers the second question, by providing the signal to take proactive action to recover buffer (See figure 1-8). If the buffer is in the yellow (middle) region, the project team should develop plans to recover buffer. If the buffer penetration moves into the red (upper) region, the project team should implement the planned buffer recovery actions. This approach causes the project team to focus on the tasks delaying the project, vs. those that might earn the most 'value.' Figure 1-8 also shows the trend of buffer penetration, enabling anticipatory action and easy determination of the efficacy of buffer recovery action.

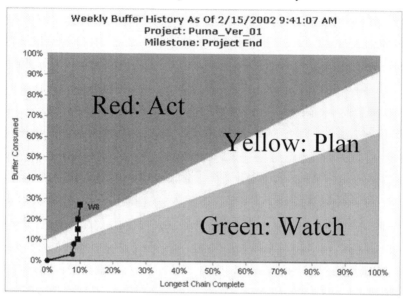

Figure 1-8: The *fever chart* visual control signals the project team when to take action to recover buffer.

Pulling the Critical Chain (Multiple Projects)

The TOC focusing steps identifying, exploiting, and subordinating to the constraint apply directly to manage projects in the multi-project environment. They implement the idea of pulling work to the constraint at its processing capability. Lean manufacturing uses the same approach for production processes.

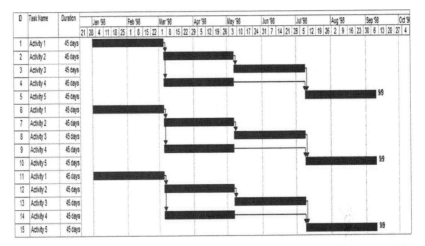

Figure 1-9: A multi-project plan with resources allocated 1/3 to each project.

Consider the multi-project system illustrated by figure 1-9. Resources share their time across the three projects. This causes all project tasks to take more than three times as long as they need to. Multi-project LPM *Identifies* the multi-project constraint as the most used resource across all of the projects, and staggers the projects so resources can work 100% on any task they are assigned to, like the runners in a relay race. Pipelining adjusts the start of projects so the resources can move from project task to project task as needed to make the whole system of projects flow to the capacity of the constraint resource.

The management team has to first identify the company capacity constraint resource. This is most often a certain type of person, but may be a physical or even a policy constraint. The company constraint resource becomes the 'drum' for scheduling multiple projects. This terminology comes from the TOC production methodology, where the drum sets the beat for the entire factory. Here, the drum set the beat for all of the company projects. Think of the drummer on a galleon. What happens if even one rower gets out of beat?

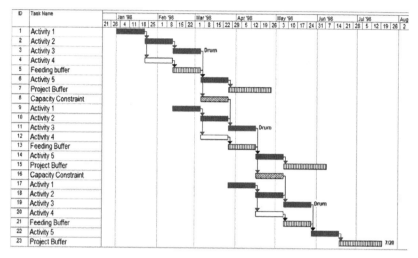

Figure 1-10: LPM pipelines projects to the capacity of the drum resource (Activity 3 resource), so resources can focus on one task at a time, and all projects can finish earlier.

The project system becomes a 'pull' system because the drum schedule determines the sequencing of projects. Management pulls projects forward in time if the drum completes project work early. Delays could affect subsequent projects when the drum is late. For this reason, projects in a multi-project environment also require buffers to protect the drum…to ensure that they never starve the capacity constraint for work. LPM schedules the projects to ensure that they are ready to use the drum resource, should it become available early.

Note that LPM does not attempt to schedule all resources across all projects. The reason is that such schedules change every day as the project tasks vary. The schedule can never provide task level start and stop dates. It is essential to determine the right task to work on based on the actual results to date. Thus, attempting to schedule into the future for all resources is meaningless. Dynamically answering the question of "Which task to work on next" also makes it unnecessary.

Synchronizing the projects to a single drum resource reduces resource contention for all resources; not just the drum resource. The example actually eliminated contention between resources for all projects because the projects are identical. While most multi-project environments do not have identical projects, synchronizing projects to the drum usually reduces a significant amount of the resource contention in the plans, even if it does not eliminate all apparent cross-project resource contention.

The reason there will be sufficient capacity for all resources with this approach is that the drum resource is the most loaded resource across all of the projects. Leveling across projects for the most loaded resource allows sufficient time for the other resources, which have excess overall capacity, to complete their work. This does not prevent actual conflicts for any of the resources, including the drum resource. It simply ensures that there is enough time to resolve those conflicts and keep to the scheduled completion date. Buffer status provides a tool to decide "Which task to work on next?" resolving the conflict for the resources. When they have more than one task available to work, they work on the one causing the most project buffer penetration.

Project Pipelining: Big Rocks First

LPM requires management to determine how to pipeline projects through the project delivery system. A given mix of projects may cause a resource to constrain the availability of your system to deliver the projects you have selected; at least adjusting the time you should plan to start the projects. As illustrated above for multi-project LPM, you need to sequence the projects to keep the individual project durations as short as possible. LPM sequences projects using a process called pipelining. Pipelining creates a schedule for the drum resource (that resource which sets the beat for the whole project system) for all of the projects, and then translates that back to schedules for each individual project. The master scheduler levels the work for *only* the drum resource across all of the projects. He/she does not level the work for other resources across all projects.

There is an urban legend about a science professor who provided a demonstration to his class. He put a very large glass jar on the lab bench, and put some large rocks into it. He asked the students, "Is it full?" They answered, "Yes." He then picked up a can filled with small pebbles, and poured them in around the big rocks. He asked again, "Is it full?" The students, getting the idea, smiled and said, "Yes, *now* it's full." He then picked up a can with sand in it, poured the sand in around the pebbles, and asked again, "Is it full?" The students, now a little worried, tentatively answered "Yes" again. Finally, in the version I like best, he picked up a large bottle of beer, and poured it into the jar, telling the students, "*Now* it is full. The purpose of this demonstration is to show that there is always room for beer." No, the purpose was to show that what at first appears to be a full system might not be full. The same will be true for your project delivery system as you add projects to it. You can often add more projects that do not use much of the drum resource without affecting all of the other projects.

All projects are not created equally. Projects that you have committed to clients are usually more important than internal improvement projects. Yet, both types of projects may compete for the same resources within you company. One way of reconciling the priority conflict is to use the matrix presented in table 1-2 for types of projects to guide placing projects in the drum schedule. First overall priority should go to those projects for which you have company commitments. You can fit the other projects in around them.

Table 1-2: An approach to entering projects into the drum schedule.

	Date-driven	ASAP
External	Priority I *Big Rocks: first access to drum.*	Priority II. *T/C sequence.*
Internal	Priority III *As necessary.*	Priority IV *T/C sequence.*

There may also be some relatively high priority projects that you have to do (e.g. regulatory requirement, broken infrastructure, obsolete software), but do not have an identifiable return on investment. Those should be priority 3 initially, but may move up to priority 2 if they cannot meet the need dates as priority 3.

You may then use your risk adjusted ranking to put the projects into the drum schedule. You can use a risk adjusted Return on Investment (ROI) (Leach 2005, 379-382) to select the projects, or you can re-rank the projects you have selected in terms of the amount of *T*hroughput they will use relative to the amount of the drum resource (*C*onstraint) they demand, i.e. *T/C* ratio.

Figure 1-11 illustrates a TOC scheduling tool used to perform project pipelining. The Concerto software (www. Realization.com) uses Microsoft Project™ to plan each individual project as a critical chain project, and then provides an easy to use tool to insert projects into the multi-project schedule and estimate the impact on all of the projects in the system.

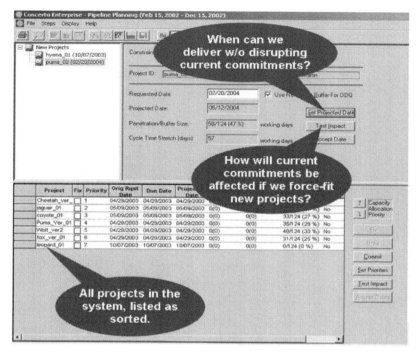

Figure 1-11: The Concerto software pipelining tool schedules multiple projects. (Used courtesy of Realization, Inc.)

Special Cases

Most organizations have some level of special case considerations that make the ROI approach difficult. Examples include:

- o Projects driven by regulatory requirements,

- o Performing required facility, equipment, or software upgrades due to obsolescence or growth needs, and

- o The need to keep a product development pipeline full at several stages to not run out of new products in the future.

Applying the TOC focusing steps and/or *Thinking Process*, and keeping the goal of the organization in mind helps to handle special cases. The other principles in this book address many of these issues, and you will be able to develop answers to your specific issues using the LPM principles.

TOC Portfolio Management

TOC portfolio management seeks to complete projects as soon as possible, and answer management's two questions:

- o   *"When are you going to be done?"*

- o   *"How much is it going to cost?"*

Portfolio management also requires continuous assurance that the project benefit is going to be achieved. The following demonstrates how TOC seeks to answer those questions operationally with forward looking action decisions.

When are you going to be done?

Figure 1-12 illustrates the primary method used by LPM to track schedule performance on a portfolio of projects. Project tracking must be timely to aid the operational purposes of project management. Portfolio managers need insight to the performance of each individual project. A table usually accompanies figure 1-12, providing the current projected completion date for each project compared to the scheduled completion (i.e. when the project buffer would be 100% consumed). This directly answers the question asked.

Projects that are in the green (lower region) are doing fine, and require no management attention. Projects in the yellow (middle region) should be creating buffer recovery plans. Projects in the red (upper region) should be implementing buffer recovery plans. Note that projects with buffer penetration less than 100% may still be on track to complete on time. Management should drill down for projects in the red to examine the trends and efficacy of the buffer recovery actions.

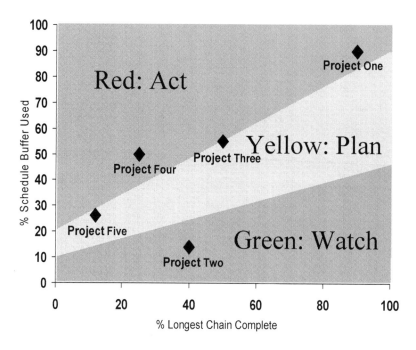

Figure 1-12: LPM simplifies viewing progress on a project portfolio, highlighting those requiring buffer recover action.

How much is it going to cost?

For some types of projects, the TOC approach clarifies that project investment cost is much less important than previously thought. For example, the impact of completing new product development projects as soon as possible to gain the first to market advantage usually far outweighs the cost to accelerate the project. However, in certain situations and for certain types of projects, cost can be important. For example, a company doing primarily fixed price projects on contract can make or lose money based on project cost.

When project cost is important, the earned value method of comparing actual cost to estimated cost becomes necessary. The reason is that schedule influences actual cost. Understanding how a project is performing on cost relative to the estimate requires removing the confounding effect of schedule because a project may appear to be over or under on cost, but may actually be ahead or behind on schedule.

For this purpose, you should use a cost buffer (Leach, 2004, pp. 174-179). The cost buffer is the cost equivalent to the schedule buffers previously described. There should be one cost buffer for the project. The total project estimate is the sum of the task estimates plus the cost buffer. You should estimate the cost buffer considering the cost variation of each of the project cost elements.

You can track cost buffer penetration using the same graphics presented above for schedule buffer tracking. The only difference required is to change the horizontal axis to represent percentage of the task budget expended. You can use both the single project trend version of the chart (Figure 1-8), and the multi-project point version (Figure 1-12).

You should estimate cost buffer penetration as a percentage of the cost buffer consumed. A project management tool called earned value cost variance (CV) is the amount of cost buffer consumed. Using the cost buffer this way is an excellent example of combining conventional project management methods with LPM.

Schedule and cost buffer tracking sometimes give contrary indications. For example, you may be in the red on both cost and schedule. Some options to accelerate schedule may require additional expenditures. Understanding the impacts on project benefits may help you resolve such conflicts.

Defining Your Project Delivery System

Every project delivery system needs at least four elements:

1. Project Charters, defining the Vision and purpose of the project, and assigning authority to the project leader to plan the project.

2. Project Plans, laying out the entire project deliverables (starting with a Work Breakdown Structure (WBS)), responsibility assignments, and processes for achieving the entire project scope (deliverables).

3. Process for project changes.

4. Measurement and control.

The amount of formality that goes into these elements depends on the project environment, the project, and the project team.

I would prefer to end this chapter with a description of a project delivery system more detailed than that provided by figures 1-1, 1-2, 1-3 and the eight principles, but it would not be helpful. Implementing a Lean system requires tailoring the system to your needs. Consider all eight principles, your projects, and your environment to develop a system that will work for you. That system should change over time as your organization and environment change.

You will find a number of project maturity models available in the literature. They assume that there is some right (and usually complex) answer for all project systems. In my experience, that assumption is wrong. You need to design the simplest system to deliver your projects. The best system for you is not the same as the best system for some other organization.

I recommend you consider design and implementation of your system as a project. Start with a project charter, and prepare a project plan for your project system implementation project. Use the principles in this book to plan and execute that project.

You can use the Six Sigma process design tools (Pande, Neuman, and Cavanaugh) to help you design and measure performance to your process. Your design should consider how you would implement a process of ongoing improvement.

As a Project Leader, your focus should be on the relationship and flow of the parts of your project. Relationships include person-to-person, person-to-task, and task-to-task. Focus on flow means ensuring the communication and hand-offs necessary to achieve the project results. Help your racers pass on the baton.

Principle two addresses the people part of project leadership in more depth.

Summary of the First Principle

- ❏ It's the system! You must design and implement an effective project delivery system appropriate to your projects, organization, and environment.

- ❏ The project system consists of people, process, and the product, and the relationships between them.

- ❏ Some of the basics of project management are essential to all projects, but few are necessary for every project. The project leader must sort out what matters most for the project at hand.

- ❏ *Any project worth doing is worth doing fast.*

- ❏ Critical Chain Project Management gives you the tools to do projects, in *half the time, all the time.*

  - o You do not have to finish all tasks on time to finish a project on time.
  - o Sometimes you can finish sooner by starting later.
  - o Adding buffers reduces total project duration and cost.

❑ Your project system must include a process of ongoing improvement.

Discussion Questions

1. What are the projects you are currently involved in or concerned about?

2. What are the rest of the projects in the portfolio?

3. What are the major differences between LPM and how you have managed projects in the past?

4. What parts of LPM are confusing at this point?

5. Is a PMO a Project Management Office, a Program Management Office, or Portfolio Management Office, and which might the differences be?

References

Anderson, D. (2004). *Agile Management for Software Engineering.* Upper Saddle River, N.J.: Prentice Hall

Covey, S. (2004). *The 8ᵗʰ Habit.* New York: Free Press

Cusumano and Nobeoka, (1998). *Thinking Beyond Lean.* New York: The Free Press

Deming, W. (1982). Out of the Crisis. Cambridge, MA: MIT Press

Goldratt, E. (1984). *The Goal.* Great Barrington, MA: The North River Press, Inc.

Goldratt, E. (1997). *Critical Chain.* Great Barrington, MA: The North River Press, Inc.

Goldratt, E. (1990). *What is this thing called the Theory of Constraints?* Croton-on-Hudson, NY: North River Press.

Leach, L. (2004). *Critical Chain Project Management, Second Edition.* Boston: Artech House, Inc.

Leach, L. (2005). Applying the Theory of Constraints to Project portfolio Management. pp. 357-391 in Levine, H.. *Project Portfolio Management.* San Francisco: Jossey-Bass

Ohno, T. (1988). *Toyota Production System: Beyond Large-Scale Production.* Portland, OR: Productivity Press.

Pande, P., Neuman, R. and Cavanaugh, R. (2002) The Six Sigma Way Team Fieldbook. New York: McGraw-Hill

Project Management Institute. (2003) *OPM3 Organizational Project Management Maturity Model.* Newtown Square, PA: Project Management Institute, Inc.

Hersey, P., Blanchard, K., Johnson, D,_*MANAGEMENT OF ORGANIZATIONAL BEHAVIOR*, Prentice Hall, 1996

PMI. (2004). *A Guide to the Project Management Body of Knowledge, Third Edition.* Newtown Square, PA: PMI

Womack, J. and Jones, D. (1996). *Lean Thinking*: Banish Waste And Create Wealth in Your Corporation. New York: Simon and Schuster

Principle Two: Leading People

The best leaders are those the people hardly know exist.
The next best is a leader who is loved and praised.
Next comes one who is feared.
The worst one is the leader that is despised.
If you don't trust the people,
they will become untrustworthy.
The best leaders value their words, and use them sparingly.
When she has accomplished her task, the people say,
"Amazing: we did it, all by ourselves!"
Tao Te Ching, verse 17

PRINCIPLE TWO: LEADING PEOPLE

Leading all of the people with an interest in your project, the project stakeholders, to endorse project success comprises the second principle. Project leaders able to keep stakeholders actively supporting project success throughout project execution can weather most storms. The effective project leader takes the stakeholders through the predictable phases of individual and team development, and skillfully helps to solve the inevitable problems and conflicts to achieve win-win solutions for all.

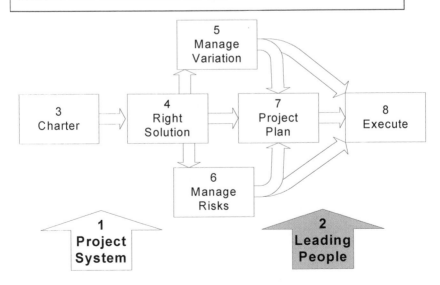

The system figure on the previous page illustrates that the second principle, like the first, underlies the others. Project management is really more about leading people than it is about managing things. This chapter leads you through the key considerations for project leadership, starting with identifying those you have to plan to lead: the project stakeholders, and ending with a powerful conflict management tool that will help you succeed with this principle.

When asked to lead a project, or decide to start a project on your own, *where do you start*? One very successful project management company (CH2MHILL, 1996) states, "The project manager's *primary* responsibility is to ensure that projects achieve client satisfaction and sound financial performance".

Although financial performance is key for many projects, internal projects are not always subject to financial constraints. However, all projects are only successful when they satisfy the customer.

I have had the advantage of reviewing some of the Project Management Office (PMO) material, and attending portions of the training of the world's best project management firms. They all focus on customer satisfaction. My answer to the question, *"Where do you start?"* is: you should start by identifying your customers, also known as project stakeholders.

40

Stakeholder Endorsement

Although CH2MHILL places the Endorsement process near the end of their book (p.159), treating it as "the final component in the planning process", they deal with it throughout the project plan development process. My experience is that if you use Stephen Covey's approach, and "begin with the end in mind", thinking about endorsement from the first time you meet your project will get your journey headed in the right direction.

The goal of project endorsement is to bring all project stakeholders to work together as a team towards the success of the project. It sets a climate of pro-active collaboration to do whatever it takes to make the project succeed. If you want to satisfy the customer for your project, a good place to start is satisfying your project team, including suppliers and all project stakeholders. You can start your project with a substantial psychological advantage by getting all of the stakeholders to physically sign up to the project Charter and Project Plan.

Critical stakeholders always include:

❑ The project client. (This is the person paying for the project.)

❑ The project team.

❑ The users of the project result.

Critical stakeholders often include regulators and others who have to approve elements of your project. They can also include critical suppliers. There may be other groups, such as business partners, financial organizations, local business organizations, unions, neighbors, human or animal rights groups, or environmental groups who can either positively or negatively affect your project. They might even include competitors.

So, why not start with a list of your project stakeholders, by name?

Then, listen to them. Ask them what they hope to get out of the project. Ask them what they believe their role is. Ask them about their commitment to project success. Covey's 5th habit comes to mind, *"Seek first to understand"*.

Think about the different levels of commitment and influence people have on a project. Then consider where you need those certain individuals to be. Now you can focus your energy to assure that you get the people you need committed to be there. Table 2-1 may help you understand where people are on the commitment scale. Someone once told me that a simpler way to think about it is a bacon and egg breakfast. The chicken is involved, but the pig is committed. You do not want any chickens in positions of key influence over your project.

Table 2-1: Commitment vs. Compliance Defines Endorsement

Commitment Comes From	Compliance Feels Like
• **Invited to participate**	• **Told what to do**
• **Goals/results driven**	• **Task/activity driven**
• **Purposeful**	• **No real value**
• **Honor-privilege to participate**	• **Participate or else**
• **Clear alignment to organizational goals**	• **Not sure why I am doing this**
• **Essential to success**	• **Something extra to do**
• **Tool to improve quality of my work**	• **Not part of my real job**
• **Collaborative team effort**	• **Monitored and inspected**

One way to plan for commitment is to use the Fig. 2-1 matrix. Put the names of each stakeholder on the grid. Put their name where you think they are on the grid, and put a dot where you need to them to be. Then, draw an arrow. From then on, focus your energy on how to move those with the longest arrows.

		Commitment	
		High	Low
Influence on Project Success	High		
	Low		

Figure 2-1: Matrix helps to determine the necessary level of project commitment, and where people are.

Endorsement is an ongoing process throughout the life of your project. You should be thinking about your project communication plan as you begin the endorsement process: find out who needs to know what during your project.

You can enhance project success with a formal endorsement session before project launch. Usually you do that in the project kick-off meeting, after your project plan is nearly complete. Nevertheless, on some projects you may need to do it early and often to keep your stakeholders aligned.

A sample agenda for a formal endorsement meeting should contain the following:

1. Define the business purpose for the project, and the purpose for the meeting (i.e. to ensure aligning everyone.)

2. Affirm the project Vision.

3. Clarify the business benefits for the project, and identify who will be accountable to ensure achievement.

4. Overview the project plan. (Early on, this may be a high level WBS and Milestone sequence (items we will build on later). For the Project Plan endorsement, it should include the detailed schedule and cost estimates as well.

5. Conclude the meeting with a verbal and written commitment by the attendees that they endorse the project.

6. Issue meeting minutes, showing who was there, and affirming their commitment to the project.

PMI defines Project Management (p. 8) as, *"the application of knowledge, skills, tools, and techniques to project activities to meet project requirements"*. I prefer to think of projects in terms of satisfying the needs of all stakeholders, which I consider more about leadership than about management. Stephen Covey (p. 100) points out that you manage things, but you lead people. He is clear that both are important, and I agree. I think you can include both in project leadership.

Leading projects involves:

1. Identifying the project stakeholders.

2. Understanding the needs of each project stakeholder in terms of the project result (product) and of the project process (e.g. communication).

3. Creating a project plan to satisfy the needs of all of the project stakeholders, including clear goals, objectives, and responsibility assignments.

4. Executing the project to achieve all of the goals and objectives.

5. Closing the project when complete.

PMI defines a number of interpersonal skills required for successful project management.

Team Building

Most of the time, your project team is newly formed. All teams go through predictable team development phases. One of the most common definitions of the phases includes the following four:

1. Forming

2. Storming

3. Norming

4. Performing

The titles of the phases (except, perhaps, for Norming) are mostly self-evident. Norming means establishing the rules by which the team will operate, both written and unwritten. Many teams never make it beyond the storming phase. Often a project leader's biggest challenge is to bring the team successfully through this phase.

Individual Leadership

Bringing a team through the storming phase requires working with each team participant. Hersey, Blanchard and Johnson's situational leadership model can help you do that. Figure 2-2 illustrates the model in terms of four levels of follower readiness (R1 through R4). Based on those levels of readiness, you use the model to vary how you treat team members; i.e. for each of the four situations (S1 through S4).

Figure 2-2 relates the Task Readiness (right to left) to the Relationship need of the follower (vertically low to high). The pair of letters in each box (e.g. HT/LR) summarizes the location, e.g. High Task, Low Relationship need. That defines the situation as S1, and the leader should take a directive style when dealing with a follower in this area. The following list outlines the appropriate leadership styles from this model, and defines the levels of readiness.

Leadership Styles

- o S1: Directive Telling
- o S2: Coaching Selling
- o S3: Supporting Participating
- o S4: Delegating

Follower Readiness

- o R1: Enthusiastic beginner: Unable and unwilling or insecure.
- o R2: Disillusioned learner: Unable, but willing or confident
- o R3: Capable but cautious: Able, but unwilling or insecure
- o R4: Self reliant achiever: Able and willing or confident

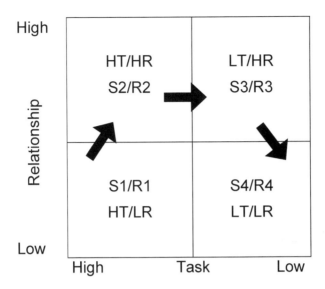

Figure 2-2: Situational Leadership Model

Keep in mind that someone at readiness level 4 for the work performed on your last project may be at readiness level 1 for the upcoming work on this project. I like to plot the project team members on Figure 2-2 from time to time, to remind myself where they are and how I should deal with them.

Two sources will help you hone your individual leadership skills. Max DePree (1989) wrote a book demonstrating that *Leadership is an Art*. He defines leadership as *"liberating people to do what is required of them in the most effective and humane way possible."* If you start with this view, you will find your leadership task much more rewarding. I highly recommend that you buy his book and keep it with you for when times get difficult on your project. He will help you look at things in an entirely different light than many leaders tend to do.

I recommend Warren Bennis to you as the final source for leadership knowledge. He has authored many leadership books, perhaps more than any author, and is best known for his distinctions between management and leadership. You can start with any of his books, but if you need a suggestion, *Why Leaders Can't Lead* is as good as any. In this work, Bennis specifically addresses "*the problems facing anyone who tries to take charge of an organization, of whatever kind, and effect change*". That is, all project leaders.

Team Leadership

Now, consider bringing the previous two thoughts together (i.e. team development and individual readiness) relative to project teams. The principle one discussion defined projects as unique. In addition, most project teams are unique; i.e. that particular group of people is coming together to work on one project for one time. (You can extend this thought to the entire group of project stakeholders as well, but we will focus here on the project team). Thus, you have a number of people who do not know each other, have no trust in each other, and have a variety of skills relative to the expected tasks they are to perform on the project. Figure 2-3 illustrates a way to think about the project team.

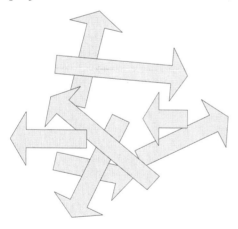

Figure 2-3a: Initial State of Project Team

The length of the arrow might represent the situational readiness of the team member, and the directions of the arrows represent their alignment towards a common goal. Initially, you do not know either for many of the team members.

The first thing you need to do is clarify the goal, and see if you can get them all headed in more or less the same direction. One of the better ways to do this is to get them to work on the project Charter, and to develop the project vision. The project vision provides a goal that they all share in common. They may not all be enamored with the specific goal, but simply by virtue of being on the project team, they do share it. You have begun to move your team through the forming phase, but have done little to bring them to know how they are going to work together, and nothing to build trust between them, and between each of them and yourself. Worse, by defining a goal some of them might align with better than others, you may have set up the situation for team storming, as they begin to maneuver to define their role in the social group. The overlapping arrows illustrate some of that ambiguity. Also, note that the arrows are still not completely aligned: they will probably never be completely aligned, as each individual is interacting with their own personal systems as well as with your project system, thus are being pulled in various directions.

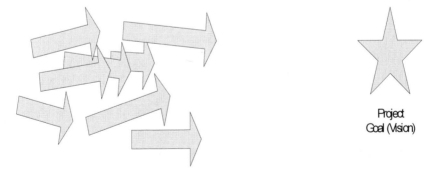

Figure 2-3b: Aligning the team towards a Goal.

Having the team aligned as in figure 2-3b does not mean it is going anywhere, and does not provide a speed; just a general direction. The speed is going to depend on how well you can match the individual team member strengths to the needs of the tasks, and ensure that there is mutual coordination between the team members. You need to provide the thrust to the group; which will begin to bring about Norming; where they have learned how to work with each other towards a common goal.

Often, as a project manager, you do not have the ability to influence the capabilities of the people on your team. They may not work for you, or even for your company, and they may be moving on to another project before you could have any significant effect on their performance abilities. On larger projects, you may not even deal with many of the performing resources directly, and instead work through their managers. This means you have to carefully align people or group capabilities with the task expectations, and ensure effective communication between them. That may be the best you can do.

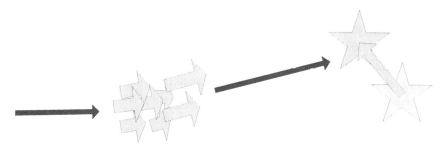

Figure 2-3c: Leading the team towards the goal requires a dynamic effort.

As the team starts performing and moving towards the goal, there will be obstacles that come up and the direction will, from time to time, drift from the intended direction. The goal might even change in some important detail (a scope change). You have to function as the captain of a ship heading towards a distant shore; assuring not only the navigation, but also the logistics (i.e. that you had enough fuel and supplies on board to start), and the ongoing maintenance and operation of the ship's systems. This will help to carry you as quickly as possible towards your goal, despite the storms and navigational obstacles that arise.

The main points I hope to leave you with from this illustration are that:

1. Every project team requires a focus on team building at the beginning.

2. The project leader must continuously focus on aligning the roles of team members with the demands of the project.

3. Team leadership is dynamic and continues throughout the life of the project.

Relating back to the quotation at the start of this chapter, even though a successful team will feel that they did it themselves, do not forget to thank them all and provide positive feedback for their hard work. When you do that, you will build positive karma for your future projects. People will eagerly want to join and work on your projects in the future. Begin your project leadership with that end in mind.

Project Roles

Project teams come in many forms and sizes, equal to the variety of the projects that they contribute. Companies use many different titles for the various roles that project team members play. Whatever name you apply to them, there are certain roles you need to foster to make your project a success. The minimum roles are:

1. Project Leader

2. Task Manager

3. Resource (i.e. the person or persons who do the work)

Larger projects may also include:

4. Resource (Functional) Manager

5. Work Package Manager

6. Project Manager/Scheduler

These latter functions exist in all projects, but smaller projects often combine the Project Leader and Project Manager/Scheduler and the Task Manager/Work Package Manager. Then, of course, there are the other project stakeholders, for example the customer for the project (the one who is paying), the users of the project result, regulators of many types, neighbors, public, and so forth: anyone with an interest in your project. I will discuss the key roles in some depth and the other roles more generally.

Project Leader/Manager Role

The Project Leader/Manager is the primary person accountable for project success. The leader's authority must match that accountability, although in many organization structures that authority may not measure up to some expectations in terms of matching responsibility and accountability. To modify a phrase I have heard often from military associate, you cannot delegate accountability. If you are accountable for something, you do not diminish that accountability by making others accountable to you for parts of it. Some apply this same reasoning to responsibility.

Some organizations designate both a Project Leader and a Project Manager (a very bad idea, in my view). In those cases, sometimes the Project Leader is more of a project technical lead, and Project Managers are available to manage the technical aspects of project planning and control. The following discussion assumes that the Project Leader performs both functions.

The Project Leader controls the project value stream. The Project Leader usually first drafts and, along with the client, approves the project Charter which, among other things, appoints the Project Leader. Then the Project Leader must create an effective plan for the project. The Project Leader creates and maintains project endorsement.

If you extend your work to deliver Lean projects to the strategic, technical, and organizational domains addressed by Cusumano and Nobekoka, the Project Leader will spend more and more time and effort working with other Project Leaders to coordinate and control the cross-project functions. In some organizations, effectively performing these roles requires a new level of multi-project executives, sometimes called Program Managers. I hasten to add, though, that many organizations understanding of Programs and Program Managers does not extend to the coordination across other Programs, as the Cusumano and Nobeoka model does.

During execution, the Project Leader has to answer the primary project control question, "When should I take action to recover buffer?" The Project Leader also must ensure smooth handoffs between the Task Managers to maintain the flow of work, and aid the project team in communicating and problem solving. The Project Leader also controls project changes.

In addition to the LPM buffer report driven decisions, the Project Leader determines how to deliver technical quality on time and for or under the estimated cost. Project level operational decisions that the Project Leader must make include:

- Disposition material that is not up to specifications. (This includes, for R&D projects, not getting the hoped for result.)

- Approve or disapprove requests for additional time or money to complete activities.

- Resolve requests to add scope. (Some day, some project may even have a request to reduce scope!)

- Resolve unanticipated resource conflicts.

- Accelerate or recover from late activities that may threaten the delivery date.

- Respond to unanticipated external influences; e.g. accidents, weather, new regulations, and unfulfilled assumptions (e.g., soil conditions dictate a need to put in pilings before construction).

- Recovery from mistakes.

The Project Leader should monitor the Project Buffer (PB) and each Feeding Buffer (FB) at the appropriate time intervals for the project, usually daily but at least weekly. For buffer management to be fully useful, the buffer monitoring time must be at least as frequent as the shortest task duration. If the buffers are negative (i.e., latest activity on the chain is early relative to schedule date) or less than the red buffer penetration criteria, the project manager should not act on the project. If the buffer penetrates between the yellow and red thresholds, the project manager should watch closely and plan actions for the buffer penetrating chains to accelerate the current or future tasks and recover the buffer. If the buffer penetrates by more than the red criteria, the project manager should implement the planned buffer recovery action. This process provides a unique anticipatory project management tool with clear decision criteria.

Buffer reporting relies on realistic estimates of how many days remain to complete a task, or remaining duration (RDU). This approach counters a tendency to report "on schedule" until the due date arrives. Project Leaders should question task status estimates that are repeatedly *on schedule*.

The Project Leader should use plotted trends of buffer utilization. The trend shows the rate of buffer consumption by plotting buffer consumed vs. critical chain accomplished. The buffer measure then acts as a control chart, and the Project Manager can use similar action rules. That is, any penetration of the red zone requires action. Four points trending successively towards the red zone require action. Trending is especially important if your processes to produce project tasks are not in statistical control. Shewhart (1986) notes, that the trend information is even more important in such cases. Most LPM schedule tools automate this process for you.

Task Manager Role

The Task Manager's job is to maintain project flow. The information the Task Manager needs is, *"Which task do I work on next?"* The trick is to work on the tasks that will move the project towards completion as soon as possible. LPM does not schedule task start dates, but instead uses buffer management to issue task assignments dynamically. Although LPM uses resource leveling to determine the overall duration necessary to complete the project, do not make the subtle deterministic thinking mistake by assuming that the resulting task dates are when tasks will take place. Tasks will start when the predecessor is complete and the resource is available, and complete as soon as possible.

As resources complete tasks, the Task Managers should put available resources to work on the next task that is a) available to start (i.e. the predecessor has completed), and b) causing the most *project* buffer penetration. This is true within a project, and across multiple projects. That task can be on or off the critical chain. In a multi-project environment, project buffer penetration can be higher on a lower-priority project. In that case, the resource should work on the task on the lower priority project before working on the higher priority project. Project priority is implicit in the start and end dates of the pipelined projects.

You can greatly facilitate this decision by providing the Task Manager with a prioritized task list, listing the tasks in the priority order in which they should start. You can automate this process with some non-LPM software. For example, a recent client using Primavera™ instituted a script to generate the prioritized list. The list put the in-progress tasks at the top, and then prioritized using a float calculation from a working schedule in which the Feeding Buffer durations had been reduced to zero. The list sorted from least float (including most negative) to most, and had a column to identify the completed predecessor task.

LPM software takes different approaches to showing tasks that are ready to work. The CCPM+ software takes a graphical approach, showing the tasks that are ready to work, in priority order. The Concerto software automates the process for multiple projects, providing the task manager a prioritized list of tasks designed to facilitate rapid task statusing and communication. We will look at these later.

The Concerto software takes a strongly user-focused perspective to provide near real-time reporting of project information. The WEB enabled software allows anyone with permission to access it anytime, anywhere. Task managers can input task status at the end of their shift in just a few minutes. Most projects that use it run the buffer analysis daily; more intense multi-shift projects sometimes run the analysis twice a day. A systems administrator authorizes different user roles, all accessing the same database. This ensures all stakeholders operate from the same data. Alternative analyses and views into the data support the different decisions necessary for the different roles.

During project execution, the Task Manager plays the key role in making the whole LPM system work: reporting task start and completion, and estimating remaining duration (RDU) for in-progress tasks. The estimate of remaining duration drives the determination of buffer penetration, and therefore can influence everyone's task priority. Task managers must be competent and committed to make realistic estimates, and must be accountable to input RDU estimates to the schedule software in time for the project meetings. Trained Task Managers take whatever action necessary to enter information on time, no matter where they may be or what they are doing.

For delivery of the task result, the buck stops with The Task Manager. There are no excuses for a Task Manager. No matter what happens to the resources or change requests on the task, the Task Manager is accountable to deliver the task result in the shortest time possible. If resources are not available or ineffective, the Task Manager must take whatever action necessary to resolve that problem. If, at any time, the Task Managers feels unable to resolve a problem to move the task to completion; they must immediately engage the help of the Project Manager and, if appropriate, Resource Managers.

Resource Role

The project resources are the people who actually do the work on tasks to create the project deliverables. The first rule of LPM implements relay racer task performance: "Once you start a task, complete it as soon as possible". They are responsible to create quality task results as soon as possible, and to pass on the results to the successor task.

Resource Manager Role

Resource Managers provide qualified resources to do the project work. Resource Managers frequently also function as Task Managers. Resource Managers often fulfill a strategic role, ensuring that appropriately skilled resources are available as needed on an enterprise and project level. The manager of the drum resource may also act as the Master Scheduler for the organization, developing and maintaining the drum schedule.

Resource Managers can use outputs of schedule programs to support performing their role. Microsoft Project™ provides a resource graph, giving the Resource Manager a view of the long-term demands on a particular resource. Most scheduling software also supports filtering for the tasks that use a particular resource. The filter works with a variety of views, including the Gantt view. This allows the Resource Manager to see the upcoming tasks. Some LPM software enhances the views and functionality of resource manager views.

Additional Roles

You can define many additional roles for your project stakeholders. The amount of effort you have to put into this depends on the project and its environment. Hostile environments and complex projects demand substantial role clarification before the project begins. Simple projects in friendly environments require very little. A cardinal rule for role definition that applies to all of these roles is clarity. RACI represents a tool sometimes used to define roles in project environments. The RACI standard roles are:

> R = Responsible (usually to do the work)
>
> A = Accountable (the one to congratulate when it succeeds, and blame when it does not.)
>
> C = Consulted (Someone who's approval is necessary to proceed or accept the results.)
>
> I = Inform (People who you should let know what happened.)

Figure 2-4 illustrates an example for a set of project stakeholders.

#	Item	Project Client	Project Leader	Project Scheduler	Project Administrator	Work Package Manager	Resource Manager	Task Manager	Resource	Senior Management	Contractors
										Stakeholder	
1	Project Charter	A	R	I	I	I	I	I	I	I	
2	Project Plan	A	R	I	I	I	I	I	I	I	
3	Project Processes		A	I	R	I	C	I	I	I	I
4	Project Requirements	A,R	C	I		C	C	I			I
5	Project Scope Statement		A	R		C	C				I
6	Project Change Log		A	C	R	I	I	I	I	I	I
7	Project Risk Registry		A	C		C	C	C		I	I
8	Project Schedule		A	R	I	C	C	I	I	I	I
9	Project Budget	A	R	I	I	C	C			I	I

Figure 2-4: Responsibility matrix illustrates responsibility by role.

You will encounter a matrix very much like this later when we address assigning responsibilities to the Work Breakdown Structure (WBS). When used for that purpose, some call it a Linear Responsibility Matrix.

Conflict Management

Team skills determine your success as a member of the human community. Team skills determine your happiness and the happiness of those around you. You use team skills every time you interact with another person. The diversity that enables teams to produce more than the sum of their parts also causes conflict. Many people consider conflict a universally bad thing, but there is another way to think about it. Conflict over ideas can be productive when it leads to developing improvements. People apply a number of strategies to deal with conflict

(Thompson, Aranda, Robbins, and others). They range from forcing their ideas on others to ignoring the existence of conflict. Figure 2-5 depicts a predictable set of outcomes depending on the way you approach conflict, and the way the other side of the conflict responds. The left column lists the approach you initiate, and the top row lists the response mode your opponent chooses. Each box predicts the probable result, both in terms of the type of resolution that will ensue and whether each side wins (W) or loses (L). In this context, win or lose is in terms of each side's position.

	Problem Solving	Forcing	Compromise	Smooth	Withdraw
Problem Solving	Problem Solving (WW)	Forcing or PS (WW or WL)	Problem Solving (WW)	Problem Solving (WW)	Problem Solving (WW)
Forcing	Forcing (WL)	Stalemate (LL)	Forcing (WL)	Forcing (WL)	Forcing (WL)
Compromise	Problem Solving (WW)	Forcing (WL)	Compromise (LL)	Compromise (LL)	Compromise (LL)
Smooth	Problem Solving (WW)	Forcing (WL)	Compromise (LL)	Smooth (LL)	Smooth (LL)
Withdraw	Problem Solving (WW)	Forcing (WL)	Compromise (LL)	Smooth (LL)	Withdraw (LL)

Figure 2-5: Conflict management Strategies Create Predictable Results (After Adams, 1997, p 203)

Unless you are in a power position to dictate outcomes, your best play is always to take the problem solving, or win-win approach to resolve conflict. Avoiding and smoothing always lead to the conflict reappearing, usually in an escalated form. Forcing can only cause compliance; it will never motivate people to higher levels of team performance.

Even this carefully thought out and widely presented approach to conflict hides a fundamental flaw. The flaw is the idea that only one side can win while the other side loses. That is, the model includes an inherent assumption of a zero-sum game. While everyone agrees that a Win/Win solution can produce a better deal for both parties, they often lose the concept during problem solving. In those cases, tools such as the figure 2-4 model often fail to help people work towards that better deal.

Stephen Covey's 7 habits of highly effective people (Covey, 1990) covers important habits for leading team performance: **Win-Win**, **Seek First to Understand**, and **Synergize**. The meaning of win-win described above aligns completely with Dr. Covey's meaning, *"Win-win is a frame of mind and heart that constantly seeks mutual benefit in all human interactions"* (p 113).

Seek first to understand is a highly important leadership trait, and an effective tool in conflict prevention and management. Covey notes, *"Most credibility problems begin with perception differences"* (p 86). The idea is simple enough: be sure you understand another person's view on a situation before you attempt to explain your view. You will learn the most this way. The *Evaporating Cloud* tool discussed below helps you do this.

Synergy is the effect that teams produce when the total team output exceeds the sum of the inputs that each member could achieve alone. It works by valuing our differences. Synergy happens when team members are able to build on each other's strengths and compensate for each other's weaknesses. The feedback in such performing teams increases the learning of the team members, further enhancing team effectiveness.

Dr. Eliyahu Goldratt developed a conflict resolution tool that I have subsequently applied to a wide range of personal and business conflicts, and found to be very powerful. The *Evaporating Cloud* (Goldratt, 1994) tool guides creation of true win-win solutions.

The Evaporating Cloud functions to *create* new solutions. Thus, it has an infinite number of possible outcomes. Some people confuse the construction to mean that the Evaporating Cloud only applies to binary decisions, or two potential choices. That is a serious misunderstanding of the Evaporating Cloud. When you have multiple seemingly equally attractive or unattractive alternatives available to you, the Evaporating Cloud can help you develop an improved solution that resolves a conflict underlying all of the alternatives.

Goldratt's Evaporating Cloud model assumes that both parties in a conflict must share a common goal. If they do not share a goal, there is no need for the conflict; so both sides could walk away from it. The heart of the Evaporating Cloud process is to convert the situation from me vs. you to you and me against the problem. This is the problem-solving approach depicted above, but now we have a process and tool to carry out the conflict resolution. (I have often found that sharing this understanding is sufficient to resolve some otherwise highly emotional conflicts.)

Goldratt also asserts that both sides in a conflict are rational. Each believes that the result they want is the best way to achieve the goal. They are like the six blind men describing an elephant based on the part they feel. They are all right, they are just considering different aspects of the whole reality. In a conflict, both sides believe they are right: they have differing positions on how to achieve the common goal. Therefore, the solution must lie in what has not been stated; i.e. the logic by which they connect their position to the common goal, or, more likely, assumptions that underlie that logic. People usually do not articulate their assumptions when working to solve problems.

Figure 2-6 depicts the generic Evaporating Cloud model. The process to use the model starts with blocks D and D'...the two opposing positions that define the conflict. These can be in the form of X vs. Not X, or in the form of X vs. Y. Next, you work to identify the common goal that both sides of the conflict share. This common goal goes in block A. In a business, it is usually quite simple to define the common goal in terms of the overall good of the business. It is a good idea to work to bring this goal down to the lowest level that both sides of the conflict can agree with.

If your conflict is not emotional, or if it involves group problem solving, you can work to develop the problem model together. If it is emotional, you will want to develop it to a point, but then you will have to take it to the other party to complete.

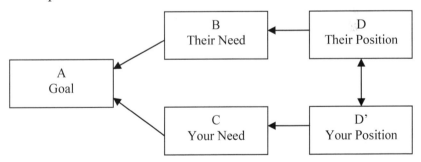

Figure 2-6: The Evaporating Cloud Model Diagrams Conflicts.

The second phase of using the model begins the search for solution, but you will have to first assure that you have properly presented the other sides position, have their agreement on the common goal, and accept whatever they tell you is their connecting logic (Block B). You should not argue with block B, but you should both check the logic of the Cloud by reading it aloud as follows:

"In order to have A, I must have B."

"In order to have B, I must have D."

"In order to have A, I must have C."

"In order to have C, I must have D'."

"D and D' are in conflict."

Now that you have agreement on the problem, you can begin to work to develop the solution. The way to do that is to recognize and expose the *assumptions* under each of the arrows in the evaporating cloud diagram. Both sides should work to identify one or more assumptions under each arrow. The road to the win-win solution is through these assumptions. You will look for actions you can take or results you can cause that will *invalidate* one or more of the assumptions, enabling both sides to achieve the goal and their individual needs, without regard to what the initial positions were. A solution that delivers the goal and satisfies both needs is a win-win solution.

You should check the evaporating cloud assumptions by reading them aloud as well. Remember that assumptions tie to the relationships between the blocks on the model...they tie to the arrows. Insert the word '*because*' when reading an assumption. For example, "In order to have B, I must have D because of *assumption*."

I have successfully used the Evaporating Cloud to make many personal decisions (e.g. whether to take a job, whether to move, major purchases). I have also used it to make many work decisions (develop or purchase a commercial software package.) I use it when facilitating teams to determine organizational strategies, and to resolve conflicts over the technical solutions to project problems. You should experiment with it on personal conflicts and non-emotional low-risk conflicts to build your skill with its development and use.

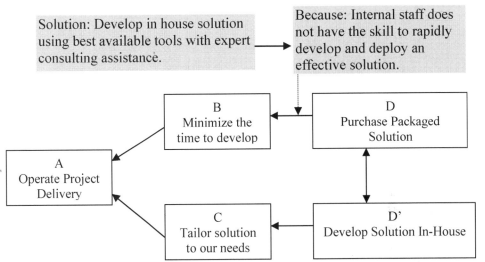

Figure 2-7: Using The Evaporating Cloud To Resolve a Make/Buy Conflict

Figure 2-7 illustrates one application I used of the Evaporating Cloud a few years ago. I was setting up the Project Management Office (PMO) process for the application development department of a major IT organization. They had a few reasonably good project mangers with effective parts of an overall process, but many unskilled project managers who had no tools and little project leadership knowledge or skill (most were excellent programmers).

The selected solution had other benefits: using tools that successfully applied on other in-house projects reduced the resistance to deploying them. The consultant we hired was able to help fill in the process and develop training that was much more tailored to this organization than a purchased product would have been. The overall cost was much lower, and overall implementation time reduced significantly.

Once you have the principles of leadership in place, you are ready to move on to your project. The next chapter covers project chartering: the necessary first step to project success.

Summary of the Second Principle

- ❏ Project stakeholders include anyone impacted by your project, positively or negatively.
- ❏ Stakeholder *endorsement* is your key to project success.
- ❏ Your project team members are key stakeholders in your project.
    - ○ All teams go through predictable phases.
    - ○ Effective team leadership can navigate the team phases towards performing.
    - ○ Responsibility assignment helps teams perform.
    - ○ Situational matching of team member skill should determine your leadership style.
- ❏ Conflicts will arise in projects.
    - ○ Effective project leaders will always use win/win problem solving methods such as the *Evaporating Cloud* to move the project towards its goal.

Discussion Questions:

1. When assigned as a Project Leader, what is the first thing you should do?

2. How can you apply the Lean principles outlined in chapter 1 to project leadership?

3. Where are you on the situational leadership grid relative to your current position?

4. Where are the rest of your team members, either relative to you as their leader, or relative to your boss as the leader?

5. What development phase is your current team in?

6. Can you describe examples of teams in each of the team development phases?

7. Use the Evaporating Cloud to identify a conflict, and then work with another person to simulate the other party to create at least one win-win solution. Use a recent real conflict you have had to deal with (preferably between two people).

    a. Identify the opposing positions as D and D', with D as your want (position).

    b. Come up with a common goal (A) both sides would likely agree to.

    c. Identify the need (B) that links your want D to the goal.

    d. The other student proposes the need that connects the goal to the others position C. (You each need to identify and conflict, and act as the 'other' on someone else's conflict.)

    e. Jointly identify at least one assumption per arrow; i.e. B_>A, C->A, D->B, D'->C, and D-D'.

    f. Identify at least one solution that will evaporate the cloud; i.e. give you A, B, and C.

    g. Discuss your thoughts on the process.

8. Complete the Figure 2-1 matrix for a project you are working, will work on, or have worked on. Include the arrows for the key stakeholders.

9. For the *long arrows* on figure 2-1, list the things you can do to move them from where they are to where you need them to be.

References

Bennis, W. (1989). *Why Leaders Can't Lead: The Unconscious Conspiracy Continues*. San Francisco: Jossey-Bass

CH2MHILL. (1996). *Project Delivery System: a System and Process for Benchmark Performance*. Denver: CH2MHILL

CCPM+ Software. Downloaded from http://www.advanced-projects.com/CCPM+.htm June, 2004

Concerto Software, url: www.Realization.com, June, 2004

Covey, Stephen (1990). *Principle Centered Leadership*. Provo, Utah: Institute for Principle Centered Leadership

Cusumano and Nobeoka, (1998). *Thinking Beyond Lean*. New York: The Free Press

DePree, M. (1989) *Leadership is an Art*. New York: Doubleday

Goldratt, Eliyahu M. (1994) *Its Not Luck*. Great Barrington, MA: North River Press

Ireland, L. (1991). *Quality Management for Projects and Programs*. Upper Darby, PA: PMI

Project Management Institute. (2004) *A Guide to the Project Management Body of Knowledge, Third Edition*. Upper Darby, PA: PMI

Shewhart, W. (1986, originally published in 1939). *Statistical Method from the Viewpoint of Quality Control*. New York: Dover Publications

Thompson, Aranda, Robbins and others. (2000). *Tools for Teams*. University of Phoenix.

A journey of a thousand miles
begins with a single step.
Confucius

PRINCIPLE THREE: CHARTERING

Establishing a project ***Vision*** and gaining alignment on a project charter enables your project team to succeed. Your project charter will be as good as the business case it puts forth, demonstrating how the project will help achieve the company goal through financial, customer, process or employee results. The project chartering phase is the best time to establish an effective process to identify and resolve the many issues and actions that will arise during your project.

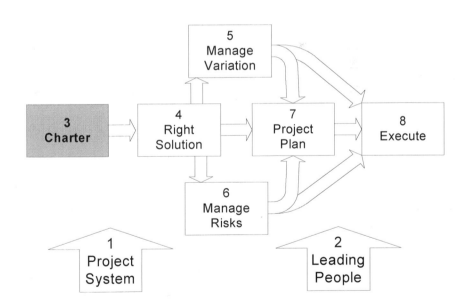

The project charter starts the process for planning and executing a successful Lean project. This chapter provides the content and process approach to develop an effective charter, including the key tools you will need to be effective.

The first thing you have to do if assigned as a Project Leader is to get an approved project Charter for your project. Your policy should be no Charter, no project. Even if it is an ongoing project, if it does not have a Charter, write one. Then work to get all project stakeholders to agree to it.

If they cannot agree to a single Charter (and a single Project Leader), look for something different to spend your time on. You are not likely to succeed on that project. The charter is your authorization as the Project Leader. It may contain a number of other things, but the thing it must contain is your authority to plan the project.

Projects arise in different ways. If you are responding to customer specifications, you often have a good definition of project scope before you start anything on the project. In such cases, your primary tasks are to be sure you deliver what the customer wants and that you control changes to that scope along the way. One good adage for such projects is, "Read the contract every day".

Gray and Larsen (2002) provide a definition of a project: "*a complex, non-routine, one-time effort limited by time, budget, resources, and performance specifications designed to meet customer needs*". This definition aligns with the definition accepted by the Project Management Institute (PMI), included in the PMBOK® Guide. The text then describes the characteristics of projects:

Characteristics of a project

1. An established objective.

2. A defined life span with a beginning and end.

3. Usually, the involvement of several departments or professionals.

4. Typically, doing something that has never been done.

5. Specific time, cost, and performance measurements.

project vs. process

Defining a project helps determine the appropriate management tools. Writers frequently contrast projects with processes. Processes violate some of the above criterion, notably 2 and 4, and generally are described, operated, and measured differently from projects. Another way to distinguish between a process and a project is that companies use process to create multiple copies of deliverables, whereas a project usually has a unique deliverable. Between these extremes are a continuum of custom manufacturing or custom construction projects that may produce many deliverables, each different from the others, but following pretty much the same project steps.

Categorization of projects as external vs. internal can be useful to determining which projects to do. Companies perform external projects for customers, expecting them to lead directly to profit. Construction projects may represent the most common form of this type of project.

Companies perform internal projects to create profit for the firm directly through new products or indirectly through improving some internal functions of the firm, or through improving some relationship between the firm and customers. ex. Information Technology projects comprise a common example of the first sub-type of internal projects. Common examples of the second sub-category of internal projects include building new facilities, installing new manufacturing processes, major product launches, or advertising campaigns.

The Charter

New projects start one of two ways: with an opportunity, or with a problem to solve. The project Charter is the tool to get people aligned on understanding the project. PMI (p. 81) defines the Charter as, *"the document that formally authorizes a project"*. I prefer to think of the Charter as authorizing the team to prepare the detailed Project Plan. Approval of the Project Plan is the formal authorization of the project. With this approach, a project charter should be no longer than three pages: one page is best. The key elements I include in a project charter (mostly from Leach, 2004, p. 108) are:

- ❑ Vision: For the project, a mental Polaroid of the project result.

- ❑ Purpose: Of the project, why are we doing it?

- ❑ Membership: Of the team to prepare the project plan, including assigning the Project Leader.

- ❑ Organizational linkage: What parts of the organization are involved in the project, and whom do the key members report to?

- ❑ Boundaries: What is in the project, what is out?

- ❑ Key assumptions and constraints.

- ❑ Team and individual responsibilities: For creating the Project Plan.

- ❑ Measures of success: For the project.

- ❑ Operating guidelines: For the project planning team.

Figure 3-1 illustrates a form for a one-page project charter containing most of the above information. Your projects are likely to require different information to meet the needs of your organization. If you use the project charter for project selection, it will likely require additional supporting information on the assumed solution; perhaps even a feasibility study or conceptual design. I recommend that you have a two-step project approval process, where approval of the charter is the authorization to create the project plan, and approval of the project plan comprises actual project approval.

Project Charter	
Project Name: **Date:**	
Project Vision (End State):	**Business Case:**
	Customer:
Purpose (Why?):	*Process:*
	Employee:
Assumptions and Constraints:	*Financial:* *Estimated Return:* *$x,xxx $\pm$ w* *$/year* *Duration of Returns:* *years* *Estimated Project Cost:* *$ y,yyy + z* *ROI: XXX $\pm$ Y*
Project Organization Linkage:	**Team and Individual Responsibility:**
Measures of Success:	**Operating Guidelines:**
Approvals:	
	Project Leader *Client/Sponsor*

Figure 3-1: Example project charter form.

You should make your project charters available to all project stakeholders. Sometimes it helps to put them on a file server. It may even be useful to you to put them in a database.

Often organizations put forth considerable effort to estimate the project cost at the chartering stage, but give little or no consideration to the project benefits. Some consider project risks as they may affect project cost or duration, and overlook the risk of achieving the stated project benefits. Please be sure to support your benefit and cost estimates with consistent approaches that provide realistic risk estimates of both the cost and the benefit.

Vision

A shared vision is a statement that creates a picture of the future project result. A project vision must be clear enough to set direction. It must be broad enough to give meaning to everyone. It must answer the question, *what do we want to create?* Key steps in the process to create an effective project vision are to:

- ❑ Understand client's mission, goals, and Strategic Plan.

- ❑ Define the mission (purpose) and goals of this project (How does this project fit in?)

- ❑ Determine the client's mental Polaroid of the project's end product (present tense).

- ❑ Link to project work scope.

- ❑ Share with project team, management, and other stakeholders.

- ❑ Review and continuously evaluate.

The vision should evoke a picture. It is even better if you can make a picture of the vision. Your discussion of the vision should always put it in the present tense, not in the future. "Our xxxx system provides customers with 90% of the services they demand within twenty seconds of logging on to our WEB site."

74

You may also wish to clarify the purpose of your projects. Purpose is the reason *why* you are doing the project. It is not a restatement of the Vision, which is the result. Here are some examples:

1. Project: New Resort.

    a. Vision: Picture of a new resort.

    b. Purpose: Capitalize on growing demand for resort services of a particular type in a particular area.

2. Project: New IT application.

    a. Vision: 30% faster client processing with zero errors.

    b. Purpose: Exceed competitor's service levels and customer satisfaction to support our business growth plans.

3. Project: Replace old instrument and control system.

    a. Vision: New digital control system.

    b. Purpose: Enhance system operating efficiency by reducing down time for instrument and control maintenance and repair and reduced system maintenance cost.

Project Assumptions and Constraints

Clarification of the assumptions you make during the conception, planning, and execution of a project helps eliminate much confusion and conflict. We always make assumptions about things, and projects are no exception. We usually think that other's assumptions will naturally align with ours. I have learned that is most often a mistake. The way to rectify that mistake is to clarify important assumptions when we make them.

At the project charter stage, assumptions often relate to the present and future conditions of the project domain, including the project stakeholders. For example, a construction project might include assumptions about the natural environment as it relates to the construction, or to the business environment as it relates to the availability and cost of materials. An IT project might need assumptions about data quality and the performance of certain hardware or software, or about the involvement of users in the project. A pharmaceutical project might include assumptions about the ability to recruit test subjects or the stability of regulations.

Constraints are entities that might limit your project. Constraints are also often assumptions, but it might help to think of them as assumptions that are out of your control; e.g. you might include a constraint to only use in-house staff to perform project work because that is your company policy. Some countries have constraints on the percentage of non-citizen workers you can employ. You may be constrained to work on some projects during certain hours of the day or days of the week. Only include constraints that you know to be real, and that will have a material affect on your project.

Business Case

Whether the project is pursuing an opportunity or solving a problem, the project must have some expected business benefit. Most companies want to know what the expected return on investment is likely to be before authorizing a project. Therefore, in addition to the expected benefit, you need an estimate of the cost that the project will generate. Management asks that most project proposals estimate the total cost of ownership (TCO) as part of the project selection process. TCO includes all the costs to complete the project, and all of the ongoing operation and maintenance cost that the project will consume over its full life cycle.

76

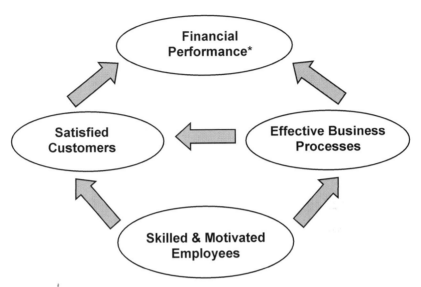

Figure 3-2: Business benefit areas and relationships.

Figure 3-2 illustrates four causally related areas through which projects can cause business benefit. The goal of a for-profit business is to make money, now and in the future. In order to make money, a business must have satisfied customers, and must have effective business processes with which to satisfy those customers and run the business. In order to both satisfy customers and run the business, all businesses must have skilled and motivated employees. The employees both run the business for today, and build the business for the future. The employees are also instrumental to transform the business to remain viable into the future. Goals in each area might include:

Financial (or other Goal)

- ❏ Return on Investment (ROI)
- ❏ Net Present Value (NPV)
- ❏ Payback Period
- ❏ Internal Rate of Return (IRR)
- ❏ Cash flow analysis

Process Goals

- Cycle time
- Availability
- Efficiency
- Persistence
- Project delivery (scope/cost/schedule)
- New product deliveries/success
- Fill in a product line
- Position Company

Customer Satisfaction

- Satisfaction surveys
- Customer Service benchmarks
  - Timeliness
  - Responsiveness
- Customer returns/complaints
- Economic value added

Employee Learning/Growth

- Employee satisfaction
- Education & training
- New employees
- Voluntary turnover
- Infrastructure
  - Age
  - Flexibility/agility

To obtain internal funding for a project, you usually must show a bottom-line financial benefit to the business, now and in the future. Therefore, although your project may focus on improving a work process, for example, you will need to relate the effect of that process improvement to the business bottom-line. I often find project teams very able to describe their project in technical terms (e.g. systems, facilities, equipment), but vague on the connection to business process improvements (e.g. efficiency or productivity improvement, or waste reduction), and lost on how that will relate to the bottom-line impact on the business (revenue, market share, profit). You can really help yourself, your project team, and your company by assuring a clear understanding of the expected business benefits of your project during the project-chartering phase.

There are only two ways to increase profit: increase revenue, or decrease cost. Increasing revenue is a far superior strategy to increase profit, because there is no upper limit to profit increase this way, and usually little chance of undesired consequences. Projects to reduce cost start with the limitation that the furthest you can possibly reduce cost is to zero. Cost reduction projects often fail to achieve the projected cost reductions. Gabor (2000) notes that management often favors cost reduction projects because they *seem* more controllable and certain (p.248).

In order to estimate the cost of the project, you must have some conception of the design approach. Often this is your first and biggest project assumption. You should be sure to clarify that it is only an assumption at this stage, and you reserve the right to look for better solutions as you progressively elaborate the project. Usually the initial design ideas that people have are far from optimal. Frequently, as soon as someone writes down an idea, others consider it carved into stone. Do everything you can to keep this from happening too soon.

You always have to make many assumptions to create a project Charter. When you do, write them down, and be sure to communicate them to all stakeholders. You are going to find them valuable as the process of progressive elaboration of your project continues.

Generally, change control is not a major issue on project Charters, as you will supersede the Charter with a Project Plan. Smaller projects can morph the project Charter into a Project Plan by adding the necessary detail. I usually make the project Charter an appendix to larger Project Plans. In any case, you will need to control changes on the Project Plan, which we will cover later.

Issue and Action Resolution

Project chartering begins the identification of many issues to be resolved and actions that must be assigned to follow up on those issues. You should start an issue and action process from the first moment you start to work on a project. It will be with you throughout the project, and you should make it your best friend. You might start with a simple table, and grow it into a database later on. Do not go into a project without an issue/action process.

You do not have to resolve issues immediately when they come up. However, you do have to capture them, and assure that you assign them to someone to resolve and close. That assigned person should acknowledge accountability for the resolution.

You can use a variety of tools to help you track issues and actions: a simple table, an Excel spreadsheet, an Access database, or a more elaborate tool (e.g. Microsoft SharePoint).

You should track the following minimal information on actions and issues:

1. Tracking number.
2. Date entered.

3. Description of issue or action.

4. Status: Open or Closed.

5. The ONE person responsible to close it.

6. The due date or completion date.

Often issue/action tracking databases contain additional information, such as the resolution or the Work Breakdown Structure number that the issue relates to (if there is one.)

I have found the following things to matter most on effective action/issue tracking processes:

1. Always *assign responsibility* for the issue *to only ONE person*. They are responsible to commit to the closure date, and do whatever is necessary to close the issue or action. They can recruit whomever they want or need to help, but only ONE person should be accountable.

2. Do NOT attempt to resolve all issues or actions when someone brings them up in meetings. Always assign someone.

3. Always get a date for resolution. If they say they cannot give you date for resolution, get a date for the date.

4. Follow up weekly on all open items.

I will close this chapter with reminding you to set up a process to support you in creating the project charter, as it will begin to serve you immediately. Once you have the charter, the next step is to define the project result. The next chapter deals with selecting the right solution for your project's requirements.

Summary of the Third Principle

- ❑ Set the Vision for the project at the outset.

- ❑ Charter your project to appoint the project leader and authorize the team to create the project plan.

- ❑ Ground the charter in the business benefit of the project.

- ❑ Begin issue and action management from the beginning.

  - o You do not have to resolve all issues when raised.

  - o You do have to assign each issue to one person to lead resolving.

Discussion Questions

1. What parts of the project Charter do you think are most difficult to arrive at?

2. How can you improve on the process to develop the difficult parts?

3. Are there additional elements that are necessary in a project Charter for your business?

4. Does your business have a template for project Charters?

5. Is there a formal process to approve and issue project Charters?

References

Gabor, A. (2000). *The Capitalist Philosophers.* New York: Three Rivers Press

Gray, C., Larson, E. (2001). *Project Management: The Managerial Process.* Boston: McGraw-Hill

PMI (2004). *A Guide to the Project Management Body of Knowledge, Third Edition.* .

Leach, L. (2004). *Critical Chan Project Management, Second Edition.* Boston: Artech House.

Principle Four: Right Solution

From the very top
You can see how all the parts
Fall into their place.

PRINCIPLE FOUR: RIGHT SOLUTION

Successful projects must deploy the right solution to the problem or opportunity that the project seeks to exploit. The right solution begins with understanding the stakeholder requirements for project success, and proceeds through translating these requirements into a successful project scope and responsibility assignment. Right solution is the primary way to reduce the eighth type of waste, products that do not meet customer's needs.

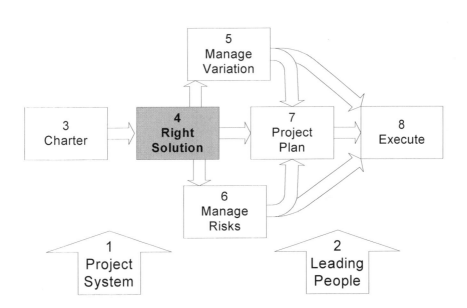

The wrong project solution is the worst possible form of project waste. Project business requirements help you define a broad solution direction, and to validate the business case for your project with that broad solution direction.

This chapter begins with determining your customer's requirements for the product that your project will produce. For some projects, that is fairly simple, as the customer provides a detailed specification; e.g. for a project that is the construction of a building or road to specifications. More often, projects begin with a broad problem or opportunity. In such cases, you must start with understanding the customer's requirements for an effective solution. Only then should you move to solution design and selection, for which the chapter presents the most effective tools I have found.

Before concluding, I discuss decision making, particularly in the context of selecting the right project solution, as well as to provide you with tools for project execution. The chapter concludes with presenting the selected design in the form of a Work Breakdown Structure and Work Packages, which will form the inputs to effective project planning.

Requirements

We are not addressing requirements for the details of facilities, hardware, or software, but rather operational and functional requirements that will deal with the business need for the project. Your project team will progressively elaborate detailed system and component requirements as you decide on a general design approach, define the project plan, and perform the design as part of executing the business system project. Business requirements must capture "*what stakeholder's expect to be able to do. that will advance their strategic, operational, or personal goals*". (Mekelburg, 2001, p. 5)

Your project documentation should describe these requirements in terms of the outcomes the stakeholders expect. Depending on your project, the form of the projects may vary. Your organization may call them requirements documents, user requirements, specifications or something else.

Mekelburg provides one of the more powerful, elegant (as in, simple) tools I have run across to state requirements. State your requirements in terms of outcomes as follows:

"[Stakeholder(s)] **expect to be able to** [business activity]"

An example she provides for an IT project is, "The insurance agents expect to be able to determine the appropriate insurance levels based on the applicant's driving record" (p. 20). A requirement for an office facility design and construction project might be, "*Company management expects to be able to increase the size of the facility in 20% increments to double the initial size without disrupting ongoing work.*" A requirement for a research project might be, "*The research committee expects to be able to make a decision on whether to proceed further on this line of research.*"

The second key point to defining requirements is to define how you will measure satisfying them. You should define the closure criteria (measures) as you develop requirements to ensure that the requirements are indeed measurable, and that you have agreement on the meaning. I have found that working to state the closure criteria (measures) while writing requirements causes me to rewrite many requirements.

The tool I have had most success with for developing and communicating requirements is the Juran (1988) requirements matrix. Although tools that are more sophisticated exist for requirements management, this spreadsheet-based tool has proven sufficient for a wide variety of projects. Figure 4-1 illustrates the roadmap Juran provides for deploying the tool through the point of defining business requirements (p.15). For those of you interested in such things, Juran's approach falls under the general title of Quality Function Deployment (QFD).

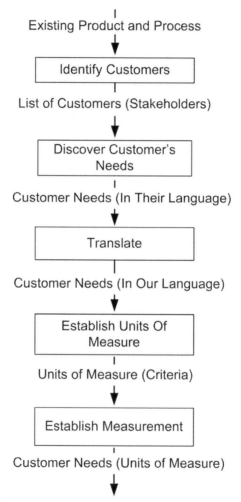

Figure 4-1: The Juran Quality Planning Roadmap

Table 4-2 illustrates a simplified single level matrix of requirements and measures, following the method that Juran uses to deploy the roadmap. (This is for a Project Plan software product I developed.) I use Excel to create the matrix, as it is easy to revise, including adding rows. Mekelburg uses Access databases. Excellent commercial products are available. Juran recommends that the matrix allow for a hierarchy of requirements. The idea is that you can first start with an overall business requirement; e.g. automate the order taking process, and then develop that requirement at lower levels of detail. Juran suggests using up to three hierarchical levels. You do not have to break down all requirements to three levels: do so only when it makes sense. When using a hierarchy, I usually copy the higher-level requirement into level two and three if there is no further detail to keep the spreadsheet populated. This allows the translated requirement to have a one-to-one relationship with a requirement.

Table 4-2: Simplified Juran Requirements Matrix

Number	Requirement	Unit of Measure	Sensor	Criteria
1	Project owners expect to be able to identify the complete project scope.	Elements of delivered scope (artifacts and services).	Project owner approval.	Project owner approves the WBS at a level identifying all deliverables.
2	Project owners expect to be able to understand the project schedule.	Dates	Project Milestone Sequence Chart.	Key deliverables have an associated delivery date.
3	Project stakeholders expect to be able to identify the elements of the budget.	Dollars	Budget table.	All deliverables have an associated budget.

The requirements in the matrix communicate with the customers (stakeholders), and thus must be in their language. You may want to convert or translate those requirements into technical language to facilitate identifying the measurements, or transition to the operations phase of the project and project closure criteria.

For IT projects, the Software Engineering Institute's Capability Maturity Model (CMM) considers requirements one of the level 2 process areas; i.e. one of the fundamentals. They establish two goals for requirements management (CMU, 1994, p. 126):

1. System requirements allocated to software are controlled to establish a baseline for software engineering and management use.

2. Software plans, products, and activities are kept consistent with the system requirements allocated to software.

I think the idea of requirement 'allocated to software' is very useful in the context of the business system requirements. An entire IT system may include facilities, people, and hardware; the software may not be called upon to deliver all of the customer outcomes.

Please be sure to focus on the *functional* and *operational* requirements of the business or hardware system. System developers frequently make the mistake of wanting to create detailed system specifications too early in the process. At the system requirements stage, you should maintain the maximum flexibility as to the direction of the solution, and thus avoid developing requirements that are really product specifications. The product specifications will be part of the system design, developed during project execution. Some of the modern flexible development processes create the detailed specifications in parallel with or after the prototypes are developed.

Solution Design

Figure 4-2 continues Figure 4-1. This figure maps where you are going with overall project definition. Glossing over this step comprises the primary weakness of many design solutions. People often seize on the first workable solution that comes to mind, rather than build an effective solution to satisfy the problem or opportunity need. On the other hand, if your project is to build something to a client's specifications, you can move directly to the plan to build it.

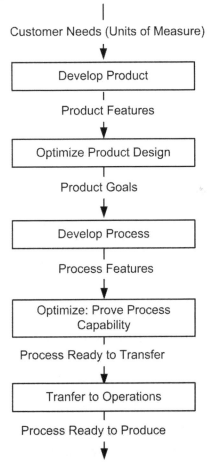

Customer Needs (Units of Measure)

Develop Product

Product Features

Optimize Product Design

Product Goals

Develop Process

Process Features

Optimize: Prove Process Capability

Process Ready to Transfer

Tranfer to Operations

Process Ready to Produce

Figure 4-2: Juran Quality Design Flowchart

On IT projects, developers often feel pressure to begin coding their solution. Keane calls this the WISCY (Whiskey) problem: "Why isn't someone coding yet?" (Keane, 1995, p. 18) Most of the time, selecting a solution direction without a comprehensive trade study is a poor solution. Once a solution direction is committed to, it is very difficult to turn back. As a Project Leader, this is the most leverage you will ever have to create a successful solution. You must ensure that a broad range of alternatives are developed and considered before you select the solution direction. You have many steps between requirements and somebody starting to build a solution, be it software or hardware.

The alternatives you consider may first include broad solution directions, such as purchase of a Commercial-Off-The-Shelf (COTS) technology, purchase of a customized tool, or in-house development. Within each of these (and probably other) broad alternatives, you can consider the System Development Life Cycle (SDLC). For example, you may be developing a new product, and have to design, test, and improve upon a number of prototypes before you can select one for final design. Alternatively, you may have a more conventional construction project, where you can design, build, and then test in a more predictable fashion.

The following sections describe the tools I have found most powerful for the design stage of projects.

Breakthrough Thinking

Nadler and Hibino (1994) define seven principles for creative problem solving:

1. Uniqueness,
2. Purposes,
3. Solution-After-Next
4. Systems

5. Limited Information Collection,

6. People Design, and

7. Betterment Timeline.

They assert applying these principles creates much better solutions, and overcomes many of the obstacles to effective solution finding. The Limited Information Collection Principle provides one principle frequently necessary to illustrate the Breakthrough Thinking approach.

The Limited Information Collection Principle asserts you should not become an expert about the data or even the problem, but rather focus your research to support the decisions you must make. I have seen the effects of ignoring this simple principle many times. It often occurs in the selection of projects.

I recently investigated the effectiveness of a project taken on a few years earlier by a major U.S. Insurance company. The purpose of the project was to reduce the cost of mailing out forms to all of their agents around the country. Rising mail prices, increasing numbers of forms, and increasing numbers of agencies added to a rapidly rising mail cost exceeding several million dollars per year. They performed an extensive study of form printing and mail costs. Careful cost-benefit analysis evaluated alternative ways of providing the electronic forms and contracting for software. They selected and successfully deployed an approach to make forms available to agents over the Internet, at a cost of several million dollars. Two years later, mail costs had gone up even higher, and the maintenance costs on the software were increasing. The Insurance Company asked me to investigate.

The first thing I did was to visit the warehouse where the forms were stored and shipped from, to look at the forms in question, and talk to the people there. I found it was not possible to convert many of the forms to electronic form; some consisted of simply colored pieces of paper cut to proper dimensions, and others were elaborate foldouts not amenable to printing on PC printers. I also found that the incremental cost of adding a few forms to any shipment was minimal, after putting a shipment together. The forms that could not be electronically converted precluded eliminating the shipments, so making some of the forms available electronically did not significantly affect mailing cost. The cost information, cost analysis, and research were worthless. The project designers should have walked over to the warehouse. The limited information they would have gathered in the warehouse would have helped them design a useful system to provide electronic forms for those where it was appropriate.

Nadler and Hibino list the purposes of the Limited Information Collection Principle as:

- ❑ To focus efforts on collecting only the necessary information for a particular project.

- ❑ To provide meaning to the existing information.

- ❑ To encourage networking for obtaining information, contacts, and results.

- ❑ To avoid disorganization.

- ❑ To lessen the preparation of many unneeded and unread documents and the arguments over differing measurement, interpretations, and analyses.

- ❑ To avoid the institutionalization of information collection as an end in itself without regard to purposes.

- ❑ To maximize the use of time, effort, and resources.

The Limited Information Collection principle is one of the most powerful tools of Breakthrough thinking. The other six principles are also very worthwhile and you owe it to yourself and your projects to learn how to apply them.

Critical Thinking

While preparing to become a University of Phoenix (UOP) instructor, I was required to take a Critical Thinking (CT) course. Doing so granted access to the module for all of the UOP Critical Thinking classes. The module includes a paper that spends many pages asserting that there is no agreed-upon definition of Critical Thinking. I know this to be true, as my own recent research revealed many definitions, and little consensus. I am not going to leave you in suspense: my definition of Critical Thinking is *thinking that leads to good decisions and effective problem solutions.*

If that definition does not work for you, alternatives abound. The most official definition I can find comes from the Delphi Report (Facione, 1990, p.2):

> We understand critical thinking to be purposeful, self-regulatory judgment, which results in interpretation, analysis, evaluation, and inference, as well as explanation of the evidential, conceptual, methodological, criteriological, or contextual considerations upon which that judgment is based. CT is essential as a tool of inquiry. As such, CT is a liberating force in education and a powerful resource in one's personal and civic life. While not synonymous with good thinking, CT is a pervasive and self-rectifying human phenomenon. The ideal critical thinker is habitually inquisitive, well-informed, trustful of reason, open-minded, flexible, fair-minded in evaluation, honest in facing personal biases, prudent in making judgments, willing to reconsider, clear about issues, orderly in complex matters, diligent in seeking relevant information, reasonable in the selection of criteria, focused in inquiry, and persistent in seeking results which are as precise as the subject and the circumstances of inquiry permit. Thus, educating good critical thinkers means working toward this ideal. It combines developing CT skills with nurturing those dispositions which consistently yield useful insights and which are the basis of a rational and democratic society.

I focus on the Critical Thinking *process*. Aaron (2001) describes one process (pp. 281-287). Carter et. al. (1998) describes other processes, and provides a plethora of useful tools. The process steps I have found most important and practical, and most frequently lacking at work, are:

1. Define the problem (in terms of the goal of your system).

2. Consider the Problem from alternative viewpoints.

3. Consider (at least three) alternative solutions to the problem.

4. Establish and use clear criteria to select from the solutions you have developed.

5. Assess potential unintended consequences of your solution.

6. Assess potential implementation obstacles.

The process I see most used is *State-the-Problem→ Select-the-First Solution* that comes to mind. This usually leads to mediocre decisions and solutions, and frequently very poor ones.

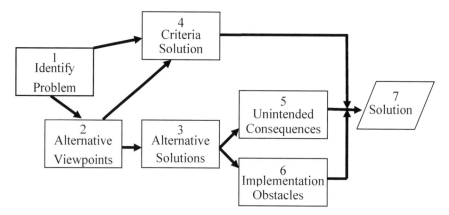

Figure 4-3: Critical Thinking Process Improves Decisions and Problem Solving

Figure 4-3 illustrates the critical thinking approach to problem solving. You can apply the same approach to decision-making. You can also use it to check the assertions made by others as to a proposed solution or decision. In that case, turn the process steps around and ask:

1. Is the problem/decision statement clear?

    a. Is it the right problem/decision to work on?

    b. Is this the right time to work on this problem/decision?

2. What alternative viewpoints could I apply to this problem/decision?

    a. Have we considered objections to each assertion posed?

    b. Have we uncovered all of the important assumptions, and asked if they are supportable?

3. Have enough alternatives been considered? Can I pose wider ranging alternatives that can provide a better short-term and long-term outcome?

4. Are the criteria for selecting the preferred alternative clear?

    a. Are they appropriate?

    b. Are they correctly weighted?

5. Have we asked the question, "*And then what?*" enough times to explore the long-term unintended consequences of the proposed action?

6. Have we assessed the potential implementation obstacles, and included mitigation actions in our implementation plan?

The process outlined above can create superior decisions and solutions. I will give you an example of it at work.

A few years ago, I lead the upgrade programs and projects at an aging nuclear reactor. This was a reactor used to produce special nuclear materials for defense purposes, and not typical of commercial nuclear power plants. This reactor discharged a fair amount of slightly radioactive water to an outside 'crib' for filtration. (To common mortals, a crib is a ditch filled with rocks.) This practice was recognized as environmentally unacceptable, so management developed a project to chemically treat the water to remove all (or most) radioactivity before discharge. The government approved the project based on a cost estimate in the range of $150 million.

When I arrived on the scene, with this project as part of my responsibility, the designers were just completing the conceptual design. They looked for alternative ways to design the facility to treat the water. Alas, their best alternative now had a cost estimate of $300 million. I helped them get agreement on the problem: Stop putting radioactivity in the crib. I then asked them to consider at least three alternatives to resolve this newly defined problem. They came back with an approach that eliminated most of the water that came from the reactor and cleaned up the water in the reactor on-line. Thus, they needed a much smaller treatment facility. The total cost of this new approach, including the modifications to the reactor system, was $90 million dollars.

Much Critical Thinking literature focuses on formal logic, logical fallacies, and thinking through puzzle problems. You can explore these aspects of critical thinking but I have rarely found these approaches used for real-world problem solving or decision-making. The exception to this is applying a set of tools using the Theory of Constraints (Dettmer, 2000). This book does not explore the *Thinking Process* method, but I encourage you to follow up on it with one or more of Dettmer's works. You may make effective use of some of the logic tools when framing and assessing formal arguments, including arguments you may make in technical papers.

Good critical thinking skills are essential for professional and academic success, including:

1. Problem-solving,

2. Making decisions,

3. Planning strategically,

4. Constructing arguments, and

5. Shifting perspectives.

Some contrast critical thinking and creative thinking, but I consider creative thinking as a necessary part of critical thinking.

When applying critical thinking most texts encourage you to use deductive (reasoning from the general to the particular) and inductive (reasoning from the particular to the general) logical arguments. Your arguments should be free of logical fallacies. Critical thinkers expect you to take alternative views, including identifying and addressing objections to your own assertions. You should disagree, but you do not have to be disagreeable.

DeBono Methods

My favorite thinker is Dr. Edward DeBono. He is most famous as the inventor of *Lateral Thinking* (1970), a creative thinking process. He does not believe it is productive to differentiate between critical thinking and creative thinking, because he emphasizes a design approach to thinking…designing better decisions and solutions. Perhaps a provocative quote on critical thinking will interest you, *"That is why the American tendency to want to teach only 'critical thinking' in schools is appalling in its medieval inadequacy"* (DeBono, 1991, p. 7).

Edward DeBono has devoted his life to improving thinking. He has authored over sixty books on the topic and has developed a host of thinking tools appropriate to different situations. The following are some design operations (1999) DeBono suggests:

❑ Move up to a broader concept.

❑ Move down to a more specific idea or concept.

❑ Consider parallels and alternatives.

❑ Perform a scan of the factors that might influence or affect the design.

❑ Challenge the basic ideas of the design (including using Lateral Thinking.)

❑ Consider fundamental changes in what you have.

❑ Modify what you have thought of so far (lesser changes than above.)

❑ Develop new ideas or approaches.

❑ Combine possible alternatives.

❑ Pick out or extract some feature, concept, or principle and build on it.

❑ Look at the context of the problem/opportunity for things to change.

❑ Pose new questions to redefine the problem.

❑ Provoke other ideas.

❑ Strengthen ideas that have been proposed, but rejected due to an objection.

❑ Make practical some seemingly impractical approaches.

❑ Analyze the problem or opportunity (i.e. break it up.)

The above list is, in reality, endless. Another method, which DeBono labeled six hats (1985), is one of his most powerful tools for solving difficult problems. Gross (1999) describes DeBono's Six Thinking Hats, a powerful tool to create solutions (p. 128-130). He designed it for use with a group, but you can use it individually as well. The basic method is to look at a problem from six different perspectives, to learn more about the problem and come up with better and more innovative solutions. The six hats are:

- ❏ **Blue**: The organizing hat, to lead the process.
- ❏ **White**: The Dragnet hat, "just the facts, nothing but the facts."
- ❏ **Yellow**: The logical positive hat, "What are all the cool things about this problem/opportunity".
- ❏ **Red**: The emotional hat. "How do we feel about this problem, opportunity, or situation?"
- ❏ **Black**: The critical or negative hat, "What is wrong with this or that?"
- ❏ **Green**: The creative hat, "What would happen if we tried…?"

The blue hat sets out the process so that all of the participants in the problem solving / opportunity session cover all of the hats. The session facilitator is responsible to collect all the data developed, and assure action assignments for follow-up. The particular path through the hats varies with the problem and how the session goes. You may visit several hats several times, but you should keep the group focused on one hat at a time to gain the full results of the process.

TRIZ

The name TRIZ derives from the Russian acronym for *Theory of Solving Inventive Problems*, developed by G. Altshuller (1992). Altshuller studied worldwide patents over many years, categorizing the kinds of solutions that made real breakthroughs (a small faction of the overall patents). He found that real breakthroughs come from overcoming design contradictions, and set out to systemize an approach to do so.

As part of TRIZ, Altshuller put forth an *Algorithm of solving inventive problems*, AZIZ. He initially identified a seven-step process to apply what he learned about developing inventive solutions. The seven steps are high-level steps, with over fifty detailed steps under them. It may seem like an oxymoron to have a process to cause inventions, but TRIZ users have developed many successes using it. Of course, it could be that some otherwise inventive people are attracted to TRIZ, or simply that people attracted to TRIZ are working on problems that require inventive solutions, and surely a few must succeed. In any case, TRIZ provides an alternative when your stuck, when people say, *"There is only one way to do it"*. That statement is *never* correct in general, but it is always true that person will not find another solution, because they have convinced themselves to stop looking. Some (there are 27 in the initial list, 40 at present) of the provocations TRIZ leads you to consider include:

- ❑ Do it inversely.
- ❑ Change the state of the physical property.
- ❑ Do it in advance.
- ❑ Do a little less.
- ❑ Separate conflicts in time or space.
- ❑ Fragment, consolidate.
- ❑ Self-service.

The Ideal Final Result (IFR) concept provides considerable stimulation to the search for better solutions.

Many people find TRIZ daunting, and some have developed more simplified approaches. Indeed, most people seem to find any creative thinking process daunting, and prefer to go ahead with the first solution that comes to mind (usually a poor one.) You owe it to your stakeholders to invest in techniques like TRIZ when the cost or consequences of your project are large.

Solution Selection

In parallel with developing alternative solution paths, you should develop the criteria you will use to select a preferred solution direction. For technologically new or risky projects, your selection criteria must also consider the risk of successful development. Usually at least three risk impacts are important: technical risk (ability to deliver the functionality), cost, and schedule risk.

Solution recommendations usually use a weighted criteria table. In addition to the weighted criterion, the solution often must meet some 'Go-No Go' criteria, before you will even consider it for weighting. One method of combining the evaluation is to use a comprehensive table in a spreadsheet, with the Go-No criteria in the top rows, and the alternative evaluations in columns. You need only rank alternatives that pass the Go criterion. Figure 4-4 illustrates an example of such a table.

#	Criteria	Weight Factor	Alternative 1 Ranking	Alternative 1 Weighted Score	Alternative 2 Ranking	Alternative 2 Weighted Score	Alternative 3 Ranking	Alternative 3 Weighted Score	Alternative 4 Ranking	Alternative 4 Weighted Score	Alternative 5 Ranking	Alternative 5 Weighted Score
1	Criteria 1	G/NG	G		G		G		G		G	
2	Criteria 2	G/NG	G		G		N		G		G	
3	Criteria 3	10	5	50	10	100	7	70	5	50	5	50
4	Criteria 4	7	7	49	7	49	5	35	3	21	7	49
5	Criteria 5	7	9	63	7	49	10	70	0	0	3	21
6	Critera 6	5	3	15	7	35	7	35	10	50	7	35
7	Criteria 7	3	5	15	7	21	7	21	7	21	10	30
	Total			192		254		NA		142		185

Figure 4-4: Weighted criteria evaluation matrix to select an alternative design using Go/No Go and weighted criteria.

Note that Figure 4-4 lists each of the selection criteria in the second column, and the alternatives above the rows at the top. The first two criteria are Must criteria, meaning that an alternative must meet them to be an allowable solution. Alternatives that do not pass the must criteria (Alternative 3 in the example) are not eligible as a choice, thus you do not even have to evaluate them against the other criteria. Even if you do, as in the example, you should not compute the total as the actual total is zero: the alternative did not pass a must. Assign a weight factor to the evaluation criteria, as illustrated in column 3 above. I use a range of 1 to 10. The weighting is relative; i.e. you value a criterion ranked 10 about twice as important as one ranked five, and about three times as important as one ranked three. Then, rank each alternative relative to each criterion. Sometimes I force at least one alternative to be a 10; the one that best meets the criteria, and rank the others relatively accordingly. Use the spreadsheet to multiply the weight factor times the ranking to get the weighted score, and sum the weighted score to get a total. Be realistic about comparing totals: generally, a difference of less than 10% in ranking is within your variation.

You may evaluate alternatives as a group, or you may distribute the table to individuals, have individuals each do the ranking, and then analyze the individual inputs. You can make the analysis as simple or complex as the import of the decision demands. For example, you may use a Delphi process to explore gross differences in ranking and reach consensus before final selection.

Decision Making

You can view solution selection as one of the many decisions a project team has to make. While I have found solution selection to suffer from too quick a decision process, other project decisions either do not get made at all, or take too long to be decided. For some reason I have found this to be a very common problem in selected fields, such as pharmaceutical development.

The evaporating cloud provides a helpful tool for decisions that you can formulate as a choice between two alternatives, and for inventing new solutions to any conflict. Many decisions are difficult to formulate as one or more evaporating cloud choices. For such decisions, you can use the solution selection matrix presented above, or other techniques.

Important delayed decisions or ones subject to frequent revision are usually decisions where the outcome is uncertain. In such cases, people are reluctant to make a mistake, and thus often seek more information before deciding. Then, when new outcomes occur, they change their decisions. Ullman (2003) describes robust decision making as making decisions that are *"as insensitive as possible to the uncertainty, incompleteness, and evolution of the information they are based on"*.

PMI (2004, p. 257) describes the Expected Monetary Value (EMV) method of deciding between alternatives with uncertain outcomes. EMV is a method to help making robust decisions. It explicitly addresses uncertain outcomes, while the decision matrix and evaporating cloud do not. EMV uses a decision tree and estimates a value and probability for each decision choice and potential outcome, multiplying the probability times the value to get the EMV of that choice. Behn and Vaupel (1982) describe this method in great detail, including real decision examples of how to apply it. They extend the EMV idea to any criteria, and develop the method to account for the confidence one can assign to a probable outcome. Assigning a confidence level to a probability is necessary to compare choices where confidence varies, a key factor not addressed by PMI.

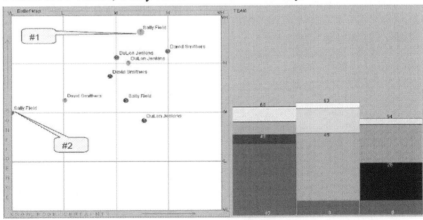

Figure 4-5: An example belief map (left) and relative ranking of three alternative solutions to a decision.

Ullman (2003, pp. 189-201) takes robust decision making a step further, addressing the confidence associated with each estimate of the outcome of a decision choice. He defines belief as *"confidence placed on an alternative's ability to meet a target set by a criterion, requirement, or specification, based on current knowledge"*. The robust decision process generates belief maps of the estimates of how well an alternative meets a criteria vs. the level of knowledge of the estimate (or estimator). Developed computer tools apply robust decision making to situations with multiple alternatives, criteria, criteria weighting, and evaluators (RDI, 2005). Figure 4-5 illustrates an example output from a decision support tool. The left side of the figure is the belief map, with the ordinate representing criteria satisfaction and the abscissa representing the confidence in the ranking. The dots represent different people's estimates. The bars on the right combine the estimates using Bayesian statistics.

Work Breakdown Structure (WBS)

After developing a general solution direction to satisfy the project requirements, you are ready to define the project scope. Project scope drives the project cost and schedule estimates. The tool of choice to organize and integrate scope is the **Work Breakdown Structure** (WBS). If you have not used a WBS in the past, I can assure you that learning to do so proficiently will be worth more than anything else in this book. The WBS is a deceptively simple appearing tool, but like many simple tools and in tune with TOC thinking, it conveys extreme power to organize, integrate, assign responsibility, and measure and control your projects.

Although a well-developed WBS looks deceptively simple, I have learned, much to my surprise, that many people have trouble creating them. If you experience some frustration with your initial attempts, do not give up. Once you become comfortable with the process, you will find them as easy to do as they are powerful.

Figure 4-6 illustrates how the WBS organizes the deliverables of the project hierarchically. The WBS does not usually reflect the sequence of work. Work Packages are intermediate levels of the WBS, and assigned to an individual Work Package Manager for estimating and performance. Work packages contain from one to a few tens of tasks. Tasks comprise the lowest level of the WBS, and are the level to develop cost and schedule duration estimates.

Your project's WBS will have different content than figure 4-6. You have to define a new WBS for nearly every project, although sometimes templates for like projects can be helpful. You should try to limit the WBS to no more than ten sub-elements, and you should work with one that is no more than three levels. Very large projects may have multiple-level WBSs, but it becomes difficult, and usually unnecessary, to manage a large WBS as a single unit.

PMI's WBS practice standard (2001) provides guidance and a number of example WBSs. The standard clarifies that the entities on the WBS should be *deliverables*. It defines a deliverable as (p. 4):

> *Any measurable, tangible, verifiable outcome, result, or item that must be produced to complete a project or part of a project. Often used more narrowly in reference to an external deliverable, which is a deliverable that is subject to approval by the project sponsor or customer.*

It often helps to think of the deliverables on the WBS in terms of the scope of artifacts (including items such as facilities, machines, and software modules) and scope of services (e.g. training, start-up operations). PMI lists the functions of the WBS as:

❑ Defining the hierarchy of deliverables.

❑ Supporting the definition of all work required to achieve the project end objective.

❑ Providing graphical picture or textual outline of the project scope.

❑ Creating a framework for all deliverables.

❑ Acting as a vehicle to integrate and assess schedule and cost performance.

❑ Associate deliverables to the responsible stakeholders.

❑ Structure project reporting and analysis.

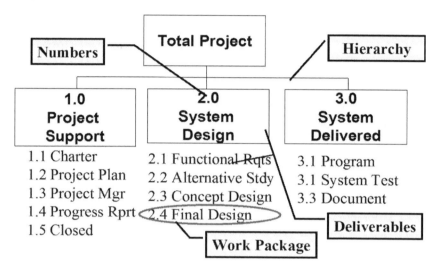

Figure 4-6: WBS Identifies Major Project Deliverables

You can use the WBS hierarchy and the RACI matrix to assign responsibility.

R = Responsible (usually to do the work)

A = Accountable *Work Package Manager* (the one to congratulate when it succeeds, and blame when it does not.)

C = Consulted (Someone who's approval is necessary to proceed or accept the results.)

I = Inform (People who you should let know what happened.)

WBS #	Deliverable	Responsibility						
		Project Leader: Sally McPherson	Design Manager: Joe Thompson	Project Scheduler: Sam Little	Project Administrator: James Triple	Project Team	Senior Management	Customer
1	Project Support	A						
1.1	Charter	A	R	I	I	I	I	I
1.2	Project Plan	A		C	R	I	C	C
1.3	Project Manager	A,R						
1.4	Progress Reports	A	R	I	C	C		I
1.5	Closed	A		I	I	I	C	R
2	System Design		A					
2.1	Functional Requirements		A	R	I	C	C	I
2.2	Alternative Study		A	I	I	C	C	

Figure 4-7: Partial example of using RACI table for project responsibility assignment.

Figure 4-7 provides a partial example for the Figure 4-6 WBS. The two key elements for completing this table are:

1. Identify every deliverable on the WBS.

2. Assign *a* person (by name) accountability for the deliverable.

The other features are optional.

Note that if you assign accountability at a higher level of the WBS, and do not assign responsibilities at levels below that, the person accountable at the higher level is accountable.

Figure 4-8 illustrates an example of using MS Project as the WBS outline and responsibility assignment tool. Note that the chart table displays the WBS number as the first column, and a contact column following the deliverable or task name. The contact at the work package level (e.g. 2.0) is the work package manager, and the contact at the task level (e.g. 1.1.1) is the task manager. When no one shows at a lower level, the higher-level person is accountable.

Figure 4-8 is an example of a project plan building work in progress. At this point, the planner has not yet assigned resources or durations to the network tasks. There are also many links necessary to complete the project network. You also have to decide how you intend to handle *Level of Effort* (LOE) and repeating tasks in the network.

Providing a project manager (WBS 1.3) is an example of an LOE task. Other LOE tasks include project administration and ongoing support such as quality, document control and configuration management, safety support, and environmental support. These resources will be present as long as the project is there. The WBS must cover them to integrate the entire cost and schedule for the project. I usually include a task for these, such as the one for the project manager. Tie the task in to the project plan completion, and show it complete as soon as assigning the project manager. You can enter the funding in as a fixed dollar amount if you wish, or if the project manager is also going to be a resource on tasks, let the funding add up from the tasks where the project manager is a resource. I do not recommend stretching the project manager task over the length of the project at some fractional person level because that can cause you difficulties later when you do resource leveling.

MS Project also allows you to put in recurring tasks, such as project reporting (WBS 1.4). I recommend you do not use your project schedule for that purpose. Specify the routine tasks in a table in your Project Plan, and communicate them as necessary; e.g. on the project WEB site.

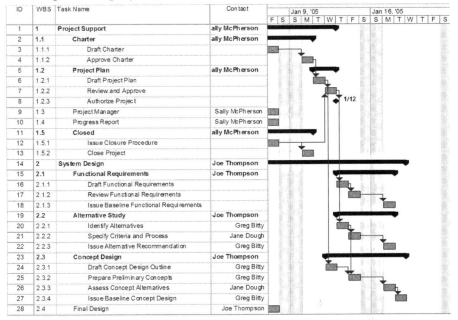

Figure 4-8: Using MS Project for the WBS outline and responsibility assignment.

Boundaries and Assumptions

Defining the scope, schedule, and cost for a project requires establishing boundaries and assumptions. Boundaries define what is in the scope of the project, and what is not. Assumptions define anything that is uncertain about reality, but has to be certain for you to make a definitive cost and schedule estimate.

Assumptions underlie every project plan. No matter how much detail you put into the project specifications, there are always lower level assumptions underlying that detail. There are always influences that could affect the course of your project, about which you have made some (often-unstated)

111

assumptions. Project plans should identify the key assumptions necessary to provide reasonable estimates of the project task parameters: resources required and task duration. For example, an assumption for a construction schedule may relate to the weather; e.g.: 'No more than six days of outside work lost due to inclement weather.' An assumption might address actions outside the direct control of the project, e.g., 'Permit review time by regulatory agency not to exceed 30 days.' You should identify these assumptions while developing the work packages.

You should also try to counter two frequent tendencies in writing assumptions. One tendency is to attempt to assume everything as a substitute for doing the necessary planning work. This may lead to long lists of assumptions, which you can summarize as, "We're not responsible for anything". Limit your assumptions to those necessary to create an effective plan. The second frequent tendency is to write assumptions in the negative; i.e., to specify what the project will not do or what is not in the scope of the project, rather than specify specific project deliverables. Cover this instead with a positive general statement that says, "Project deliverables include only the specified items."

Milestone Sequence

An effective way to aid developing the logic is to first identify the major project phases, in terms of key milestones for the project. Figure 4-9 illustrates an example of the key milestone chart structure. Each milestone must have a specific deliverable assigned to it. The milestone sequence chart does not include dates. Dates result from the integrated schedule; they are not inputs to it unless it is a project with a definitive end date, such as a proposal submission or a meeting, such as the Olympics.

You may then ask, *"What is necessary to complete each of these major milestones?"* and build a list of supporting milestones under each of the key milestones. The resulting milestone sequence chart; worked jointly by all of the key project team members, provides a basis for developing and sequencing the tasks defined in the work packages (described below). It provides many of the linkage points to tie the work packages together.

You may also use the milestone sequence as a supplemental tool for project measurement. Many organizations establish project decision 'gates,' as key points for project reviews; such as completion of the system engineering or completion of the first prototype test for development projects, or completion of the conceptual design for construction projects.

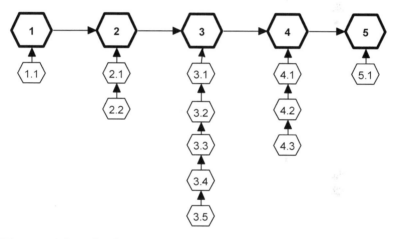

Figure 4-9: The key milestones define a 'backbone' for the project task sequences.

Creating the WBS and Milestone Sequence. Developing the WBS and Milestone sequence is always a team sport. Unless you fill all the project stakeholder roles personally, you just cannot do it in a vacuum. On larger projects, you also cannot necessarily get everyone together in one place at one time. That is fine: organize a traveling road show, and share the progressively elaborated result back to the earlier groups as you move towards a final product. The general process that I recommend (assuming you could do it in one session):

1. Start the group off to agree on a *Vision* statement for the project: what will it look like when completed. Think of it as a mental Polaroid. It helps many people if you actually create a picture.

2. Set up to collect *Assumptions, Risks,* and *Issues* that will come up during the session. Do not attempt to resolve issues in the session: capture them, make an assumption that enables you to put something on the WBS or Milestone chart, and move on.

3. Develop the *WBS* from the top down to three levels, assuring that you focus on *deliverables*. The items on the WBS should be *nouns*, not verbs.

4. Develop the *Milestone Sequence* from right to left, and then down, assuring that you capture key deliverables. Do not put dates on the Milestones. Dates come much later, if at all, for the Milestones. The only date allowed at this stage, if you have one, is a customer final need date.

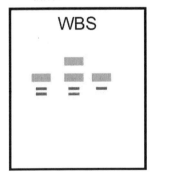
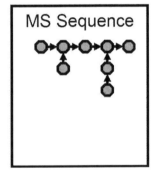

Figure 4-10: Collect the WBS and Milestones on Poster Pages

Work Packages

Work Packages provide the basis for the project network, schedule, and cost estimate. They are contracts between the Project Manager and the work performers. They are the source documents for inputs to the integrated cost schedule plan for the project. Work packages contain:

1. The scope to be delivered by the work package,
2. Specifications or reference to specifications, codes, and standards for the deliverables,
3. The activity logic,
4. Activity resource estimates, and
5. The basis for the activity resource estimates.

The next sections will cover items three through five in the above list. The design of your work package documentation can greatly influence the ease and quality of planning the project. It is the point at which many managers begin to whine about "too much paper". You must design the work package process to be simple and user friendly.

Responsibility Assignment. You must assign elements on the WBS to people to plan and manage. These individuals sometimes have a title, such as Work Package Manager, Core Team Member, or Cost Account Manager. They are usually technical experts in the subject matter of that portion of the WBS. They must define the detailed work scope, establish the task sequence, and estimate the task resource requirements. They are responsible to identify the links between their Work Packages and others in the program. They also supply the justification for the resource estimates.

Once you have selected the right solution for your project, you are ready to move towards creating the project plan. Before I describe the details of the project plan, I will take you on a short detour to ensure that you have an effective understanding of one of Dr. W. Edwards Deming's points of profound knowledge: understanding variation. Variation is the key to successfully plan and execute your project.

Summary of the Fourth Principle

❑ Requirements set the basis for solution design: be sure your stakeholders agree on them.

❑ Always develop at least three alternative solutions to the problem. Various tools can help you define and develop a solution right for your problem or opportunity:

  o Juran process.

  o Breakthrough thinking.

  o DeBono tool set.

  o TRIZ.

❑ Select the *right solution* using criteria that reflect stakeholder's requirements.

❑ The WBS, Milestone Sequence Chart, and Work Packages enable you to structure the project to execute your solution effectively.

Discussion Questions:

1. Have you worked on projects that did not have a WBS and responsibility assignment? What did the project team use to assure all work was covered?

2. Have you worked on projects where half way through, or even at the end, someone realized that there was a much better way to handle the objective?

3. Can the assignment of Work Packages and Work Package Managers help clarify roles and responsibilities for projects in an otherwise functionally organized company?

References

Altshuller, H. (1992). *And Suddenly the Inventor Appeared.* Worcester, MA: Technical Innovation Center, Ins.

Behn, R. and Vaupel, J. (1982) *Quick Analysis for Busy Decision Makers.* New York: Basic Books, Inc.

Carnegie Mellon University (CMU). (1994). *The Capability Maturity Model: Guidelines for Improving the Software Process.* Reading, MA: Addison-Wesley

Covey, S. (1989). *The 7 Habits of Highly Effective People.* New York: Simon and Schuster.

DeBono, E. (1970). *Lateral Thinking.* New York: Harper and Row

DeBono, E. (1999). *New Thinking for the New Millennium.* London: Penguin Books

DeBono, E. (1985). *Six Thinking Hats.* Toronto: Key Porter Books

Dettmer, William J. (1997). *Goldratt's Theory of Constraints: A Systems Approach to Continuous Improvement.* Milwaukee: Quality Press.

Facione, P. (1990). *Critical Thinking: A Statement of Expert Consensus for Purposes of Educational Assessment and Instruction.* Millbare, CA: California

Juran, J. (1988). *Juran on Planning for Quality.* New York: The Free Press

Keane, Inc. (1995). *Productivity Management: Keane's Project Management Approach for System Development.* Boston: Keane Inc.

Mekelburg, D. (2001). *DRIVE TO CLOSURE: MANAGING EXPECTATIONS. Extremely Successful Software Projects-Volume 1.* Personal communication from the author.

PMI. (2001). *Practice Standard for Work Breakdown Structures.* Newtown Square, PA: Project Management Institute

RDI (2005). Downloaded 1/22/05 from: http://www.robustdecisions.com/decision-management.pdf

Ullman, D. (2003). *The Mechanical Design Process.* Boston: McGraw Hill.

I returned, and saw that under the sun, that the race is not to the swift, nor the battle to the strong, neither yet riches to men of understanding, nor yet favour to men of skill; but time and chance happeneth to them all.

Ecclesiastes 9:11

PRINCIPLE FIVE: MANAGING VARIATION

Variation and uncertainty are the ways of the world: to prosper, your management must go with the flow. Managing variation requires understanding it and putting proper controls in place for the two types: buffers for common-cause variation, and risk management for special-cause variation. The four commonly used buffers are: the project buffer, feeding buffers, the capacity constraint buffer, and a cost buffer. Simple buffer sizing usually works best.

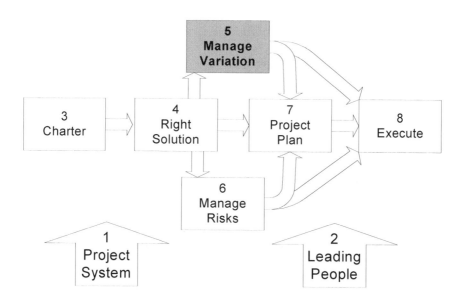

This chapter provides a definition of the two types of variation that you must manage differently to succeed with Lean Project Management. It then focuses on using Buffer Management to manage the first type of variation (common-cause), reserving the next chapter to apply project risk management to manage the second type of variation (special-cause).

Effective operation of any system requires active management of variation because, as in the quote at the start of the chapter, *chance happeneth to them all.*

Uncertainty means indefinite, indeterminate, and not certain to occur, problematical, not known beyond doubt, and/or not constant. All predications are uncertain. Fundamental physics tells us that all knowledge of reality is uncertain; the better we know the position of something, the less we know about how fast it is moving. Uncertainty is the true state of the world.

Most people use the words variation and uncertainty interchangeably. Dictionary definitions are not very helpful on the distinction. I use variation to describe getting different outputs from repeated application of the same process, and uncertainty as including our knowledge about the result: a measure of the predictability of the variation. For example, the results of any task in a project will vary if you did the same task repeatedly. Measuring this variation can produce an estimate of how much that task will vary in the future; e.g., the time or cost to produce the result will vary from project to project. You will use some method to estimate the task for a new project. That estimate will include the historical variation, and introduce some other causes of uncertainty, for example, the people that do the task next time may not be the same ones that did it last time. With this definition, uncertainty is generally greater than historical variation.

Variation

Shewhart (1986), a mentor to Dr. Deming, identified the need to operate systems in a state of statistical control in order to have a degree of predictability. He observed "Every mathematical theorem involving this mathematically undefined concept [statistical control] can then be given the following predictive form: *If you do so and so, then such and such will happen.*" In other words, your project task performance processes must be in statistical control for your project schedule to have any basis in reality.

Shewhart also notes (p. 96) an estimator who understands variation "*does not attempt to make any verifiable prediction about one single estimate; instead, he states his prediction in terms of what is going to happen in a whole sequence of estimates made under conditions specified in the operational meaning of the estimate that he chooses.*" A single point estimate, for example "two weeks for this task" has a mathematical probability of zero. Yet, people put together project plans with single point estimates for each task, and compute early and late start and finish dates for each task, and then track peoples performance to these numbers that have absolutely no meaning.

A meaningful estimate requires an operational definition of what the number means. That definition must specify a range for the number to fall within, to some level of probability. For example, "*There is a 50% chance this task will take two weeks or less*" has meaning. Almost no one specifies project task durations that way. I ask students at the beginning of my PMI seminar classes to estimate a real project task. They all comply with a single number estimate. Not even one has given a range, and no one has asked or specified what their estimate means in terms of a probability and range. They may mean a 50%

121

chance of getting it done in that time or less, and I may be wanting a duration that they can really commit to; i.e. a 90% plus probability that they will get it done in that time or less. When pressed, most people allow that the latter is kind of what they think management really wants for task estimates. If so, based on actual task data I have seen for a large number of types of tasks, the 50% estimates will be approximately one half or less. Figure 5-1 illustrates the reality of most project task estimates in terms of a statistical distribution. The contingency illustrates the difference between about a 90% probable estimate and a 50% probable estimate. It is usually on the order of a factor of two or more. If the mention of statistics bothers you, you can ignore this figure and go on.

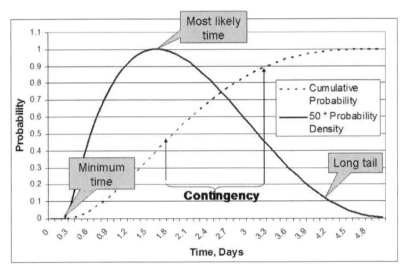

Figure 5-1: The statistical distribution of most project tasks looks something like this: a minimum time, most likely time, and no maximum. Exact prediction of any task duration is impossible.

Of course, if the numbers people are giving for task estimates do mean a 90% chance of completing the task in that time or less, than 90% of the tasks should complete in less time. That does not happen very often for a variety of reasons I put under the title of date-driven behavior. People mentally convert the dates in a project schedule to deadlines. They change their behavior and actions to try to deliver on that date, but no sooner. Thus, they systematically waste all of the early task completions. They do not think of it as waste. Sometimes, they are simply responding to the system. For example, with contracted resources paid by the hour, they usually are not paid after they turn in the result. Why would they ever own up to finishing early?

Scheduling software tends to reinforce the illusion of deterministic task start and stop dates. I see many users of MS Project and other software making printouts listing all four of the dates on tasks (early/late start/finish). If they show the Gantt chart at all, it is squished over on the right side of the page, making it impossible to see the relationships between tasks.

Keep in mind that the so called early/late start dates computed by the scheduling programs are not really early and late start dates. They are dates calculated based on a deterministic estimate for each task. The difference between early and late does not represent the variation in actual task duration, it is the result of a deterministic calculation of the parallel paths in the network.

Since I am not likely to succeed at getting Microsoft or anyone else to change their software pictures (we are still using the proven inefficient QWERTY keyboard, aren't we?), I hope instead to convince you to use what they have as logically as possible. This means, when you print out schedules, do not print out any dates for individual tasks. Print out the schedules as you see I am doing here; for example on figure 1-10. Even on large projects, you can use filtering to reduce the number of tasks that you show to a meaningful number so you can see the relationships between them.

Second, I encourage you to think of each of those task bars you see as having fuzzy front and tail ends, as illustrated below. If we use 50% probable task duration estimates, that should mean each task has at least a 50% chance of being able to start sooner than shown, and, since we are going to show the bars for the mean task length only, a 50% chance of extending beyond the end of the bar. That is going to be OK, because you will size buffers to ensure the project completes on-time or early, even with half of the tasks taking longer than their mean time.

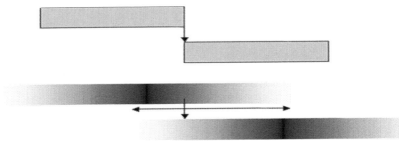

Figure 5-2: An unrealistic (upper),but usual, and better (lower) illustration of tasks in a project plan.

Figure 5-2 illustrates (upper) how most project schedule Gantt charts show tasks: as having definite start and finish times. I encourage you, whenever you see such a picture, to understand that it is a very flawed picture of the reality of variation, and that the lower picture is a more accurate representation. Even though the lower illustration is not a great depiction, as the down arrow can be significantly to the left or right of where shown. The plot thickens when a task requires input from several predecessor tasks, or requires a resource that might be working on another task. In those cases, the input from all of the predecessor tasks and the resource(s) are required to begin the successor task. Delay of any of the predecessor tasks, or delay of resource availability, will delay the start of the successor task.

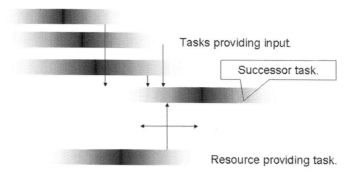

Figure 5-3: Example case of a successor task requiring inputs from three predecessors, and a resource from another task. The latest arrival determines successor task start.

Figure 5-3 illustrates a case of merging paths in a task network, where three predecessor tasks provide input to a successor task, and where the successor task needs a resource working on a task on yet another path in the project, or even on another project. If the 50% duration tasks were to represent the upper part of figure 5-2, the probability of starting the successor task would be about the multiple of 0.5*0.5*0.5*0.5, or only about 6% chance of starting on or before the task start date. No wonder people are often frustrated waiting for input!

Critical chain introduced the feeding buffer to account for the task merging situation depicted by figure 5-3. The critical chain feeding buffer follows any predecessor task not on the critical chain, buffering the variation for a successor task on the critical chain. The feeding buffer helps assure that a task on the critical chain has all of the necessary inputs at a 50% probability in order to start. Figure 5-4 illustrates two feeding buffers needed where three parallel paths join, one of which is the critical chain. Note in this case, inserting the feeding buffer introduced an apparent gap in the critical chain. Since reality is more like the depiction of figure 5-3, this gap is not a matter of concern.

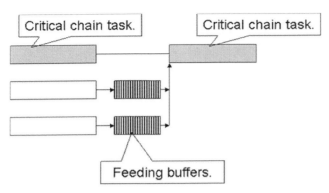

Figure 5-4: Feeding buffers inserted where non-critical chains merge into the critical chain help ensure task input availability.

Dr. Goldratt introduced the idea of a resource buffer for critical chain projects, to ensure that the critical chain task also has the resource when it is otherwise ready to start. A combination of approaches have replaced the need for a specific resource buffer. First, providing a capacity constraint buffer ensures that there is sufficient protective capacity for all internal resources. Next, the display capabilities of project software enable resource dispatching decisions to minimize delay on the critical chain. Filtering by resource and prioritizing task lists based on the effect on project completion support dispatching resources to the correct tasks. If conflicts appear to arise (i.e. a critical chain task is ready to be worked, while the resource is working on a non-critical chain task), the software helps the resources know which task to work on next. Usually, the resource should finish the working task, and then use the priority to select the next task to work on. If one of the available tasks to work on is on the critical chain, and others not, the priority will favor the critical chain task, because delays to the critical chain immediately impact the project completion. Exceptions occur if a feeding chain in the project has experienced a delay greater than its feeding buffer, which could give that task greater priority (unless the critical chain has experienced more delay).

LPM requires using resource leveling as a first cut to reduce resource conflict for tasks. In a multi-project environment, the LPM capacity constraint buffer ensures protective capacity for the most loaded resource, thus ensuring more excess capacity for other resources. These two steps, combined with a dynamic decision process for resources to determine which task to work on next, and buffer recovery actions when needed, handle the variation in resource availability.

Common-cause and Special-cause Variation

Deming emphasized the need to separate common-cause variation from special-cause variation. You must first distinguish them in order to get a system under statistical control. Common-cause variation defines the capability of a system to repeatedly produce results within mesurable parameters. Special-cause variation causes results to extend beyond that range; usually due to causes outside the system.

Consider your daily trip to work. If you time yourself for a month, you would find the actual door-to-door time varies; usually by twenty to fifty percent from the average. In other words, if the average time is 30 minutes, sometimes you might make it in 20 minutes, and sometimes it might take you 45 or 50 minutes. That would be the common-cause variation in your trip to work. You will not change that without changing the process; e.g. getting a partner so you can ride the HOV lane, take a different route, or leave for work early enough so that there is no traffic.

Sometimes, it can take a lot longer. A major snowstorm or hurricane may tie up traffic so bad it takes you hours to do what is normally a 30-minute trip. Those events are cases of special-cause variation.

This same common-cause variation persists in nearly all project tasks. Although the performing resources may have done the same or a very similar task many times before on different projects, each time it takes a different amount of time. The conditions are never exactly the same, and many other variables can cause variation in the duration of the task. While individually the causes make small differences, sometimes they can add up to quite a lot. Any time I have been able to get data on actual project tasks, I find the range necessary to cover most of the data (e.g. 95%, or 2 standard deviations for the mathematicians), approximately -50% to +100% of the mean value. For example, if a task usually takes a week, sometimes the resources can get it done in less than three days, and sometimes it will take two weeks.

Management's function is to design and operate project systems that are in statistical control, so there is some basis for predicting how long project tasks will take. Management is also responsible to operate and improve the system, while avoiding two mistakes:

> Mistake 1: Treating common-cause variation as if it were special-cause variation, and

> Mistake 2: Treating special-cause variation as if it were common-cause variation.

The reason to minimize these two mistakes (you cannot completely avoid making them some of the time) is that making the mistakes invariably increases variation in your project result.

LPM uniquely differentiates between the methods to handle common-cause variation and special-cause variation. We use buffers and active buffer management to protect the project due date from common-cause variation. The buffer acts as a control chart, separating common-cause variation from special-cause variation, telling the project team when to take action to recover buffer, and when they should not (avoiding tampering). LPM uses conventional deterministic project risk management to reduce vulnerability (probability and potential consequence of specific risks) to special-cause variation.

Effects of Variation in Projects

We are primarily concerned with the effect variation in planning and executing projects produces on project schedule performance. Recall that in Deming's (1993) four points of profound knowledge, not only do the four elements themselves matter, but also the relationships between them. This is especially true of the relationship between understanding variation and human psychology. Human beings have a number of well-known shortcomings in understanding variation (i.e. common mistakes), which relate to behavior because of the psychological effect of variation. The relationship of variation and psychology causes project waste by delaying the result of the project. The primary impacts of variation we are concerned about with planning and executing a project are the waste due to delays:

External to the Task

- ❑ Queuing. Queuing occurs when the input to work on a task is available, but the resource is engaged on another task. Just as a line builds before the server in a supermarket, a line of tasks to be worked on can build before a resource.

- ❑ De-synchronization. Resource available, but the input is not, because a predecessor task has not provided the input for the resource to work on.

Internal to the Task

- ❑ Bad Multitasking. People can usually only work on one task at a time. When they claim to be working on multiple tasks, they are actually switching back and forth between the multiple tasks. This behavior delays all of the projects. Since the value of a days delay for each of the projects is the delay of the project benefit for a day, the damage caused by bad multitasking in most organizations is immense. It is usually also

129

unknown. Many even think it is efficient to multitask. Studies show that even at the most basic level, efficiency is lost by task switching; often up to 40%. Nevertheless, the extensions of whole projects by factors of three to five are common, and much more serious. Please note that bad multitasking works at the group level is well. Pre assigning resources to project tasks at less than the most efficient number of available resources to do the task in the shortest amount of time is another form of bad multitasking.

❑ Parkinson's Law. The law states that work expands to fill the available time. In projects, the assigning of specific due dates to tasks often causes the task performers to delay handing in a completed result until the due date, wasting the potential for project acceleration, or offsetting of later task over-runs. Sometimes organizational and contractual incentives reinforce Parkinson's Law by discontinuing payment on a task once turned in as complete. In that environment, who would ever turn in a task early?

❑ Student Syndrome. Goldratt (1997) described the student syndrome as a worker waiting to start on a task until the due date seems immanent. Student syndrome wastes the potential for project result acceleration, as well as causing delay when normal variation causes the task to extend beyond the nominal duration.

Keep in mind that the daily value of delaying a project is the complete expected value of the project per day, and has nothing to do with the cost of the resource that is causing the delay. Recent projects I have worked on included pharmaceutical developments, where the ultimate value of a day earlier of the drug reaching the market could be $12 million dollars per day, and parts for an oil platform where the daily value of the oil pumped by the platform could be $10 million per day. While these may be extreme examples, the impact of delay usually far outweighs the resource cost.

The LPM principle of relay racer task performance is a first level defense against the delay wastes listed above. Relay racer task performance at the individual level means focusing on one task at a time, and passing on the result of that task as soon as completed. Relay racer task performance favorably impacts four of the five sources of waste described above. Management must create an environment for relay racer task performance by answering the question for each resource, *"Which task should I work on next?"* Buffer management provides the answer.

Buffers

Buffers distinguish the critical chain method from the critical path method. Buffers enable you to most effectively manage common-cause variation. LPM buffers include:

1. The Project Buffer: A time buffer at the end of a project critical chain.

2. Feeding Buffers: Time buffers that connect non-critical chains of tasks to the critical chain.

3. Capacity Constraint Buffer: A resource capacity buffer, used in staggering the start of projects.

4. Cost Buffer: A dollar buffer to comprise the total estimated budget for a project.

Some critical chain implementations use two additional buffers, but we will not be using them as they have limited value, or we have other ways to accomplish the intended function. The drum buffer is a buffer placed in a project to help project acceleration in case the drum resource is available early. The resource buffer is a buffer to alert resources needed for critical chain tasks that a task is coming up to be worked.

You should size Buffers to enable fixed end date and total dollar commitments to projects with high reliability, or low risk of exceeding the estimate. Buffers, when combined properly in the LPM approach, always lead to shorter total time lines and lower total dollar estimates than a non-buffered plan meant to achieve the same probability of completion. The reason is that the mathematical way that buffers concentrate risk protection requires less total protection than if it is distributed amongst the project tasks. Table 5-1 illustrates this.

Table 5-1: Total (time or cost) with buffers is always less than without, for the same probability of outcome.

Item	Low Risk Estimate	Mean Estimate
Task 1	20	10
Task 2	20	10
Task 3	20	10
Task 4	20	10
Buffer	0	20
Total	80	60

Buffer management uses buffers dynamically to help control the project. The next chapter will describe how in detail. Buffer management provides information back to task managers and resources to answer the question, *"Which task should I work on next?"* Providing this answer enables resources to engage in relay racer task performance, avoiding bad multitasking.

Buffer management also provides information to the project team on when they should take action on the project to recover buffer, and when they should not. It tells the project team exactly where to focus on to control the project. Buffer management dynamically answers two management questions:

1. *When is the project going to be done?*

2. *How much is it going to cost?*

Buffer management requires reasonably accurate statusing of project tasks with an estimate of the duration remaining to complete the task. Cost buffer management also requires timely and accurate collection of actual project cost.

Project Buffer. The project buffer is located at the end of the critical chain of a project. All chains of project tasks must merge before the project buffer. There is only one project buffer in a LPM project.

Eli Goldratt, inventor of the critical chain theory, suggested sizing the duration of tasks in a project by taking the normal estimates for the tasks, and reducing them in half, and then adding a project time buffer equal to one-half the sum of the duration of the tasks along the critical chain. Thus, the buffer comprises approximately one third of the total project time (a little less if there are gaps in the critical chain.) Goldratt constantly seeks simple solutions, and this is certainly a simple way to size a project buffer. Although skeptical at first, I have found it be an effective way also, for many projects in many project environments. Very sophisticated project organizations are unlikely to adopt this method, though, in part because it seems *too* simple.

The PERT model, devised in the 1950s, was the first model to explicitly account for task variation (PMI, 2004). PERT uses optimistic, most likely, and pessimistic estimates of task duration or cost to estimate the mean and standard deviation for each task. The PERT method assumes that the difference between the optimistic and pessimistic estimates is some multiple of the standard deviation. The method then applies the square root of the sum of the squares (SSQ) of the differences (u_i) to estimate standard deviation of the sum. Some texts recommend using this with a table of the normal distribution to estimate total duration or cost vs. probability, and to size the appropriate buffer.

Another LPM buffer sizing method uses the same statistical basis as PERT, but only two estimates for the task duration: a most likely and a low risk estimate. LPM (Leach, 2003) does not make a specific assumption about the number of standard deviations between the two numbers. It assumes that the same number of standard deviations is acceptable for the pooled result as was inherent in the task estimate ranges. The difference between these two estimates is the uncertainty, u_i, in task estimate (duration or cost). The LPM SSQ method uses the equation:

$$\text{Variation Buffer} = \sqrt{\textstyle\sum_n u_i^2}$$

n is the total number of tasks along the critical chain.

For example, consider a chain of four tasks, with low risk estimates of 20 days, and most likely estimates of ten days. The uncertainty, u, is 10 days for each task. $10^2 = 100$. n = 4. So, the variation buffer is the square root of (4 * 100), i.e. 400. The square root of 400 is 20.

Leach (2004) describes several schedule buffers and an overall project cost buffer, recommending the square root of the sum of the squares (SSQ) method to size buffers, along with a minimum project buffer size of 25% of the Critical Chain, and a 10% minimum cost buffer to account for bias. Continuing experience supports the simpler method Goldratt proposed originally: One-half of total duration of the tasks in the chain.

LPM buffer sizing recommendations follow the statistical logic used in PERT. The sizing uses two statistical facts:

1. The variance of the sum (schedule path or total cost) is the sum of the variances of the elements, i.e. task duration or cost, and

2. The Central Limit Theorem, which states that the distribution for a collection of samples will tend towards a normal distribution, regardless of the shape of the distribution the individual samples are drawn from.

LPM should use the *mean* duration and cost estimates as the baseline task estimate. The reason for this is that the mean is the only unbiased estimate of the sum along a path or for the entire project. For these techniques, the bias corrections discussed below are relative to the sum of the mean task estimates along a path, or the total sum of the elemental costs for a project. As illustrated by table 5-1, this sum will be substantially less than the sum of the pessimistic (low-risk) estimates used in basic critical path.

Real projects usually have hundreds and frequently thousands of activities. The largest projects may have tens of thousands. Schedule and cost buffers estimated by the variance pooling method become a very small percentage of the total duration and cost. As the number of activities pooled in the variance grows, the variance of the pooled mean as a percentage of the mean reduces. Whether you use PERT, the LPM SSQ method of buffer sizing or Monte Carlo simulations, you will see the same general behavior; i.e. decreasing relative total variation with increasing project size.

The PERT, Monte-Carlo, and SSQ buffer sizing methods reduce the relative size of the buffer as the number of tasks grows large. This implies that larger projects should be more likely to come in on budget and time; i.e. the trend of the model is towards increasing project success (closer to estimate) with increasing project size. However, real project data shows project success rate decreases with increasing project size. The famous Standish Group (Johnson, 1999) study calls it success that the average over-run (bias) on IT projects is down to 60%, from over 200% in 1994. It shows a strong (negative) correlation of project success with size, the opposite effect predicted by the PERT, Monte-Carlo and SSQ methods. No projects over 10 million dollars were successful. Similar results obtain for other types of projects. Thus, the predicted trend of the PERT, Monte-Carlo and LPM SSQ models do not correctly describe reality.

Leach (2003) describes the cause of this discrepancy as bias in project performance. The PERT, Monte-Carlo, and SSQ methods all assume that task variation is independent in one task from another. That is not always true: there can be reasons that many or even all tasks tend to over-run the estimate (e.g. bad weather effect on outdoor work). Leach identifies 11 additional potential causes of bias: that is, things that can make a project take longer or cost more, but not come in shorter or for less money. Bias effects add linearly, not as the square root of the sum of the squares. Therefore, Leach recommends sizing buffers using:

Project Schedule Buffer = Variation Buffer + Bias Buffer

The variation buffer uses the SSQ method described above. You can use table 5-2 to help you estimate an appropriate bias estimate for your projects if you have no historical data.

I now only recommend this method after you have operated with LPM for several years. You should start with the much simpler Goldratt approach of one-half the chain.

Table 5-2: Bias estimation guidance.

Bias Factor	Schedule Impact	Cost Impact
Omissions	Some, not to exceed cost impact	5%-10%
Merging	< 20%	None to small (controllable)
Errors	5%-25%	5%-50%
Over confidence	None	None
Queuing	LPM: Nominal (Resource leveling & capacity buffer)	No direct impact (See LOE)
Multitasking	LPM: Small (feeding buffers)	Up to 40% (efficiency loss), plus LOE impact
Special Cause Variation	0%-30%	0%-30%
Student Syndrome (Starting late)	Small (Buffer management)	None to positive
Date Driven Behavior (Not reporting early completion)	Small (Run rules)	~5%
Failure to Report Rework	0%-20%	Covered by errors
LOE	None	LOE rate times schedule delay
Total	10%-25% (Project Buffer) More with many parallel tasks	10%-25% (Cost Buffer)

Feeding Buffers. The same rules used to size project buffers apply to sizing feeding buffers. Of course, you sum for the tasks on the particular feeding chain. When feeding chains branch upstream of the point where they tie in to the critical chain, use the longest or the most uncertain chain to size the feeding buffer. Even if you choose to use a more intense calculation method to size the project buffer, you could still use the Goldratt method of one-half the chain to size the feeding buffers.

Capacity Constraint Buffer. The capacity constraint buffer assures that the resource with the highest demand to supply ratio across all of the projects in the system has sufficient capacity to do the work in the time allotted. Since all other resources have a lower demand to supply, they will have more excess capacity than the most loaded resource. You need excess capacity in a system with variation to limit the wait time to have resources available when needed. You use the capacity constraint buffer to determine the start dates of projects in a multi-project system.

Queuing theory is the mathematical tool to predict the performance of waiting lines for any situation, from the checkout in a store to calls waiting on a telephone exchange. It also helps understand project tasks waiting for resources to work on them. Simple queuing theory predicts a non-intuitive result, which probably contributes to why many project over-run their schedules. Most people assume that if the average processing rate of work equals the average arrival time of tasks, that there would be no or little waiting line.

I know most people think this because I have asked hundreds of people in my classes. So far, only one has ever got it right, and he was an expert in queuing theory. Figure 5-5 illustrates what actually happens as the utilization of a server to queue approaches one. A utilization of one means the average arrival rate equals the average processing rate. The line waiting to be served is far from zero or one: it actually grows to infinity. So does the wait time.

Line Length

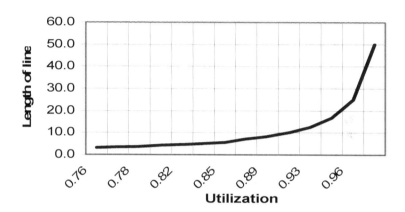

Figure 5-5: Queuing theory predicts an infinite line and wait time if task arrival rate equals task-processing rate (Utilization = 1).

In actual systems, it takes time for the line to grow, and the line can never get infinitely long. However, notice on the figure that even at a utilization of 0.85, i.e. 15% excess capacity, the average line reaches about four units. Consider that as four project tasks backed up for your critical resource to work on. Thus, the average wait time would be four times the average length of the tasks. For this reason, a capacity constraint buffer about 25% is necessary to have your system of projects flow with minimal work in progress.

Cohen, Mandelbaum, and Shtub (2004) illustrate with a simulation that sizing of the capacity constraint buffer is a trade-off between project throughput and project duration. They found that *reducing* the capacity constraint buffer from 50% to ~17% *increased* project duration by ~22%. This type of behavior roughly follows the figure 5-5 queuing curve. Further reductions in capacity constraint buffer have a proportionately large impact on project duration due to the increase in queuing time. Reducing the capacity constraint buffer also significantly increased the variation in project duration.

Even if your organization is only doing one project, you must consider the need for a capacity constraint buffer, as otherwise you may overload the critical resource on even that one project, causing queuing delay. In the case of one project, you can implement a capacity constraint buffer by having the availability of the most demanded resource at less than its actual availability. For example, if you have ten engineers, you may set the supply of engineers as nine in the resource table.

You may use an implicit capacity constraint buffer by planning conservatively relative to how you will actually deploy resources. For example, you may schedule resources for only five eight hour days, but be willing to extend the work schedule to five ten hour days...creating the effect of a 25% capacity constraint buffer.

Cost Buffer. The cost buffer performs the same function as the Project Buffer, but for cost. The discussion for the project buffer applies. The only difference is that the cost buffer sums for all tasks in the project, not just along the critical chain. The various methods for sizing the cost buffer also apply, and table 5-2 provides information to help account for bias in cost estimating. Because the cost buffer sums over all of the project tasks, the cost buffer can generally be smaller than the project buffer as a percentage of the mean estimate.

Buffer sizing is the last step of preparing your schedule and cost estimate for your project. You have two more steps to go, and you will be ready to start work! The first of these steps, covered in the next chapter, plans how to manage potential special causes of variation. Project risk management provides the tools you need for this.

Summary of the Fifth Principle

❏ Normal (common-cause) variation exists in all project tasks.

❏ The amount of common-cause variation in most project tasks is larger than many people think: on the order of -50% to +100% of the mean duration.

❏ Relay racer task performance is a key to combating the negative effects of variation.

❏ Use buffers to manage common-cause variation.

    o Project buffer.

    o Feeding buffer.

    o Capacity constraint buffer.

    o Cost buffer.

❏ Simple task and buffer sizing usually works best.

❏ Adding buffers reduces the total estimated and actual time and cost.

Discussion Questions:

1. Do your current projects use cost and schedule buffers? If so, how are they sized?

2. What do you think about needing 25% excess capacity for the most loaded resource in your organization?

3. Can you think of other potential causes of bias in schedule or cost performance on the projects you work on?

References

Cohen, I., Mandelbaum, A., Shtub, A. (2004). Multi-Project Scheduling and Control: A Process-Based Comparative Study of the Critical Chain Methodology and Some Alternatives. PM Journal, June 2004, pp. 39-49. Newtown Square, PA: Project Management Institute.

Deming, W. (1993). *The New Economics for Industry, Government, Education.* Cambridge, MA: MIT

Goldratt, E. (1997). *Critical Chain.* Great Barrington, MA: North River Press.

Johnson, J. (1999, December). *CHAOS into Success.* Software Magazine.

Leach, L. (2004). *Critical Chan Project Management, Second Edition.* Boston: Artech House.

Leach, L. (2003). *Schedule and Cost Buffer Sizing.* Project Management Journal, Newton Square, PA: Project Management Institute.

Parkinson, C. (1957). *Parkinson's Law.* Cuthogue, NY: Buccaneer Books

Project Management Institute. (2004) *A Guide to the Project Management Body of Knowledge, Third Edition.* Upper Darby, PA: PMI

Shewhart, W. (1986). *Statistical Method from the Viewpoint of Quality Control.* New York: Dover Publications.

The doctor of the future will give no medicine, but will interest her or his patients in the care of the human frame, in a proper diet, and in the cause and prevention of disease.
Thomas   Edison

PRINCIPLE SIX: PROJECT RISK MANAGEMENT

Project risk management develops actions to reduce the probability and potential undesirable consequences of identifiable (special-cause) risks to your project. Active risk management extends over the life of the project, involving risk identification, analysis, and mitigation.

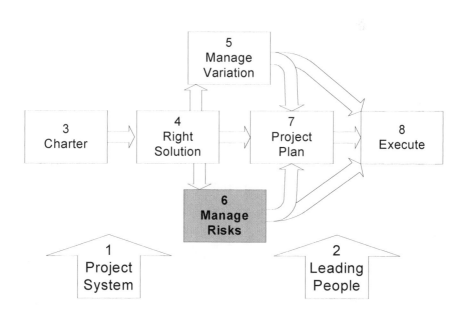

This principle defines uncertainty as different from variation, and then provides a process to manage it. *Deterministic project risk management* seeks to control these special-cause risks to project goals: scope, cost, schedule, and customer satisfaction. Other processes deal with other kinds of risks, such as health and safety risk or environmental risk. Project risk management seeks to control project risks beyond the scope of your project plan, and beyond your 'circle of control.' The project risk matrix is the primary tool to identify and manage risks.

Uncertainty

I like to define uncertainty as relating to our knowledge about the future. Table 6-1 provides a method of categorizing uncertainty that Dr. David Ullman and I have developed. It identifies three uncertainty categories, provides some examples, and suggests alternative management methods to reduce the uncertainty or manage the potential consequences. We developed these categories as an operational aid to clarify the alternative management methods.

Principle five addresses common-cause variation, and demonstrated how LPM uses buffers to estimate and control variation. LPM assumes that the project task processes are in statistical control, thus enabling a control chart type of approach. Project risk management is the way to control special-cause risks for projects: those with consequences that may extend beyond the control limits.

The second category listed in Table 6-1 is design uncertainty. Design uncertainty affects many projects, and causes both the

144

content of project tasks and the project task network itself to change. For example, in research and development projects, the design of the end product is unknown at the outset, and the tasks necessary to create the product can not be known until the design is known. The first way to handle such design uncertainty, as addressed in principle two, is the process of progressive elaboration: only planning what you know in detail. Progressive elaboration necessarily requires project change management: changing the project plan when you do know more. Principle four addressed the middle approach listed for design uncertainty: Robust decision making. This method appears little known in the world of project management. The final category marks the realm of project risk management: principle six.

Table 6-1: Various types of uncertainty and management approaches.

Type	Examples	Management Method
Variation **Common-cause**	All causes of variation within the output of products/processes in statistical control (most conventional project tasks).	Projects - Buffers and action thresholds (e.g. control charts). Products – tolerances and statistical process control.
Design Uncertainty	Lack of knowledge, assumptions, difference in opinion and viewpoint.	Progressive Elaboration Robust decision making. Project or product change management.
Environmental and Internal Uncertainty	Natural events, new regulations, external-driven changes in project requirements, accidents. Failures or changes with the product or process.	**Project risk management:** (Identify, Quantify, Monitor, Prevent and Mitigate).

Risk Management Process

PMI defines project risk as *"an uncertain event or condition that, if it occurs, has a positive or negative effect on a project's objectives"*. They outline a six step risk management process, which I believe appropriate for special-cause risks:

1. Risk management planning.

2. Risk identification.

3. Qualitative risk analysis.

4. Quantitative risk analysis.

5. Risk response planning.

6. Risk monitoring and control.

Risk management is only as valuable as the actions you take to prevent or control the potential impact of the risks you identify. You must decide on courses of action to include in your project plan based on the relative risk of these events that may or may not occur. Whenever you make a project assumption, you make a project risk decision because you assume that future reality follows your assumption. You have project risk events when your assumptions do not come true.

Project Managers have several options to deal with project risk events, including:

1. Preventing the occurrence of the risk,

2. Identifying and monitoring the risk triggers (e.g., reviewing weather forecasts and monitors),

3. Preventive actions to reduce the potential consequences of the risk, should the event occur,

4. Insurance,

5. Preparing for mitigation in case a risk event occurs, and

6. Accepting a risk.

Since LPM handles common-cause task variation, your project risk management need only deal with special-cause risks.

Risk combines two components: the probability of a risk event, and the impact to the project. Risk is the product of multiplying these two components.

Risk types include:

1. Program Risk: Risks that may cause client dissatisfaction.

2. Business Risk: Impact the project may have on the rest of the business; including financial risk and risk to the company reputation.

3. Cost Risk: Potential to impact the project cost buffer.

4. Schedule Risk: Potential to impact the project schedule buffer.

5. Health and Safety Risk: Potential for injury to the project team or public beyond the risks routinely accepted by the public.

6. Environmental Risk: Potential to affect the environment.

7. Regulatory Risk: Potential to affect the project from some regulatory impact.

Process. The process focuses on qualitative risk assessment with risk ranking because:

1. Data is usually not available to justify detailed quantitative risk assessment, and

2. Supplying probable risk numbers can yield a false sense of accuracy.

Risk Matrix

Table 6-2 shows the risk management matrix, summarizing:

❑ The risk,

❑ Assessment of the risk, and

❑ Actions to monitor, prevent, or mitigate the consequence of the risk.

Table 6-2: The Risk Matrix Example (LPM Implementation)

#	Risk Event	P	C	R	Trigger to Monitor	Prevention Actions	Mitigation Actions
1	As a result of a **work pressure** *management resistance to change* may result, which would lead to **delaying the benefits of LPM**.	3	3	9	Low management attendance at training. Lack of management leadership and/or tool implementation.	Management buy-in sessions. Senior management goal setting and follow through. Assurance of management availability and skill to use tools.	Support to management that is not leading the implementation. Remedial counseling by senior management.
2	As a result of **system incompatibilities** *the LPM software availability may be delayed*, leading to **inability to plan projects in LPM**.	2	1	2	Trouble reports.	Careful specification of system requirements. Early testing of system functionality. Buffer between installation and need.	Use of LPM software vendor to resolve incompatibilities.
3	As a result of partner lack of knowledge or willing to participate in LPM *integrated LPM plans may not be achievable*, leading to **an inability to create a drum resource schedule, and continued bad multitasking**.	2	3	6	Partner complaints.		Alternative technology
4	As a result of **frequent changes to plans** *additional planning effort may be required* increasing cost and/or **delaying useful resource schedules**.	2	2	4	Concerns/complaints that the plans do not reflect current reality.	Apply rolling-wave planning, to minimize planning rework.	Bring in additional temporary planning support. Reduce time horizon of plans.

Table Key:

P (Probability)
3 = 20-50%
2 = 5-20%
1 = < %%

C (Consequence)
3 = > Project (Time or Cost) Buffer
2 = ≥ 20% of Project Buffer, ≤ Project Buffer
1 = < 20% of Project Buffer

R = P*C

The content in the table is only for illustration; your content should be much more specific to your project. I encourage you to follow the lead of combining like risks together in order to keep the overall length of the list to a reasonable number of items (i.e. less than a 'dirty dozen' or so).

You should define what a reasonable number of items is based on the overall risk and size of your project. Relatively small projects (i.e., less than a few million dollars and under one year) should not have a risk list in excess of ten items. If your list for a project of this size really seems to have a lot more high impact, high consequence risks, you should ask yourself if you really want to do that project.

Column two in table 6-2 describes the potential risk event. You may start with a list of many specific events that people can imagine, and then lump them together for subsequent analysis. You may also categorize risks in terms of the probability and potential impact; the next two columns. That is, you may have one event for low impact natural events and another for large impact natural events. The reason to do this is that the two types of events will lead to different mitigation strategies.

Hilson (2004) provides a risk statement format that I find useful to clarify the risk statement. The format is: "As a result of **<definite cause>** *<uncertain event>* may occur, which would lead to **<effect on project objective(s)>**." I have propagated the use of bold and italics to the example risk statements in table 6-1 to illustrate how to use the format.

Columns 3, 4 and 5 provide a relative quantification of risk. Risk is the product of consequence and probability. The key below the table provides one possible way of quantifying the probability and consequence for a project. Note that the probability refers to the probability of the risk occurring during the project. This probability only goes to 50% because if you judge the probability higher than that, you should assume that the risk event would occur when preparing you project plan.

That is, risks with a probability greater than 50% should be a baseline assumption. LPM provides a unique consequence measuring stick: impact in terms of the relative impact on penetration into the project time or cost buffer. You may have additional consequence criteria, such as safety risk or public reaction risk. The recommended scale ranks risk from one to nine.

The sixth column in table 6-2 lists the 'Trigger to monitor.' This is the thing you should frequently assess to see if you should change your risk assessment, or activate your contingency plans. You should, of course, attempt to come up with 'leading indictors' whenever possible.

Columns 7 and 8 of table 6-2 are the most important; listing the actions you will take to prevent or mitigate the potential risk. Prevention and mitigation may work on either the event probability or the event impact. For example, a spill control dike reduces the potential impact of a spill, but not the probability. On the other hand, a double wall tank reduces the probability of a spill. Actions to prevent the risk should then become part of your project work-plan. Actions to mitigate may require actions in your project work-plan to plan for mitigation; such as training or purchasing emergency supplies.

Listing risks might give you ammunition to say, "I told you so". It also opens you to the question, "And why didn't you do anything about it?" You must take action on the identified risks to have any result from your risk analysis. Your actions might include:

❑ Actions to prevent (or reduce the likelihood of) the risk event (e.g., breaking the project into phases; or researching uncertain project elements to improve certainty),

❑ Transferring the risk, (e.g., subcontracting),

- ❏ Monitoring to determine if the chances of the risk are increasing (e.g., monitoring for precursors),

- ❏ Actions to reduce the consequences of the risk event, should the risk materialize,

- ❏ Insuring against the risk event, or

- ❏ Action to mitigate the consequences in the event the risk materializes.

You may choose to use a consistent approach to applying these alternatives, such as:

- ❏ Risk ranking 6-9: Assign risk to one person to monitor, and as Task Manager plan and execute preventive actions and execute activities to reduce potential impact.

- ❏ Risk ranking 3-5: Assign risk to one person to monitor and prepare to implement prevention and mitigation actions if necessary.

- ❏ Risk ranking < 3: Monitor as a group monthly at a project meeting.

Identifying Risks.

You may use a variety of methods to identify risks. One method starts with the assumptions your team felt necessary in order to develop project work estimates. Each of these assumptions represents a risk of not being true. You may use checklists, such as the one included in the Wideman's Appendix A (1992), or Pritchard (2001). You may use computer assistants, such as included in some software offerings. You may simply get your project team together, and brainstorm a list to start with (this is the approach I usually take). You may evaluate the problems encountered by previous similar projects. Coming up with the list is usually the easy part. You will never be able to predict the future, so you will never be able to come up with a 'complete' project risk list. It would be infinitely long anyway, and not very useful to your team. Instead, you should seek to obtain a representative list of the type of risks likely to confront your specific project during its time of execution.

Many of your project assumptions may translate to project risks if the assumptions do not come true. For example, your assumption that regulatory permit reviews will take 60 days low-risk and 30 days average duration may become a risk if the reviews take longer than two thirds of your project buffer. You may have reason to expect that the reviews could take much longer based on recent experience with the same regulatory agency on another project.

On the other hand, you should guard against too many project assumptions. You need to ensure that a rule of reason applies in specifying both the project assumptions and the associated risks.

Checklists. Checklists can help you identify risks you might otherwise overlook. Checklists have two inherent problems:

1. Check lists may include risks not significant to your project, but that become believable once suggested, and

2. Checklists may lead to over-confidence that you have considered everything important, limiting your search for things beyond the checklist.

Use the rule of reason.

Scrutinize your project plan, asking the question, "What could go wrong?" in each of the major steps to aid in developing your risk list. You can let this list get relatively long while preparing it, as you will consolidate it in the next step.

Group like risks to consolidate the list before developing your action plan. You should come up with a reasonable set of risk items to manage. You do not increase the accuracy of your risk list by increasing the level detail. You increase usefulness by increasing the range of the risks you consider. An infinite number of potential risk events threaten your project, but only some will happen. You could never list them all, and it would be a useless list anyway, as you could never prevent or mitigate all of the risks. Instead, work to capture the most likely and significant types of risks, and put in place the appropriate information and response system to deal with them. You can lose focus if the risk list becomes too long. Try to limit the list to, at most, ten or twenty items. For most reasonable size projects (i.e., less than ~ $ 10 million and one or two years in duration), keep the list to under ten items.

Probability of Risk

Estimate the probability of each risk event actually occurring during the life of your project, and only work on those with a reasonable probability. Do not spend valuable project resources guarding against low probability events. On the other hand, you want to work to prevent events that are likely to occur, and you should prepare to handle some unlikely events, if the potential consequence is large enough.

People have certain inherent limitations when attempting to estimate probability. Most people experience a number of well-documented logical biases and errors. People also tend to be unjustifiably confident in their erroneous 'knowledge.' The following lists the common errors.

❏ **Combining probabilities.** The probability of two independent events is the product of the probabilities of the individual events. Since probabilities are always numbers less than one, the probability of the two events is always lower than the probability of either single event.

❏ **Base rate**. The base rate error fails to consider the distribution in the population. For example, consider a bead drawn from a population of 90 % white beads, and the probability of correctly identifying a white bead in

153

dim light of 50%. A person looks at a bead under those conditions, and says 'black bead.' What is the probability that the bead was black? Most people answer 50%. The correct answer is only 5% (.1 X .05 = 5%).

❑ **Anchoring.** People stick close to initial positions put forth by others or themselves; especially concerning numbers. This bias sometimes causes groups to influence each other. If you want independent input, you have to seek independent input. Having one person review another's work does not provide independent input.

❑ **Overconfidence.** People are inherently overconfident in their estimates. Put another way, people systematically underestimate variation.

❑ **Availability**. People tend to remember what happened most recently, or famous events, and mistake them for events that are more probable. The availability error gives unjustified bias towards something thought to be 'typical', often assigning a higher probability to events that are more 'typical' because they match a stereotype.

❑ **Confirmation.** People tend to look for instances that confirm their decisions. Unfortunately, confirmatory cases have no value in scientific proof. People should look for instances that would disconfirm their hypothesis. This bias often results in worthless tests. Effective tests must always seek to disconfirm the hypothesis.

❑ **Law of large numbers**. People routinely accept small samples as indicative of a larger population; and fail to understand that the variance in small samples tends to be much larger than the variance in larger samples or the population.

❑ **Representativeness**. People mistake 'more typical' for 'more probable.' For example, people will claim that a description of a person is more likely to be 'a school teacher' than 'a working woman', based on a description that includes traits people associate with schoolteachers. Since 'working women' also includes all women schoolteachers, it is more likely that she would be a working woman than a schoolteacher.

Use this list to critically review your list of risk events and assessment of probability and impact. Ask, "Are we making this error?"

High probability. You should count on items with a greater than 50% probability as a baseline assumption. Define a high risk as less than a 50% chance of happening during the life of the project, but more than a moderate risk, which you might define as ranging from a 10% to 20% chance.

Moderate probability. Moderate probability risk events are less than high probability and greater than low probability. They are events that may occur during the life of your project, but you would not bet on them happening (or, at least, you would want very favorable odds on the bet.)

Low probability. Low probability risks includes risks unlikely to occur during the life of your project (i.e., less than a 5% chance of happening), down to a very low probability; perhaps about 1 % or less. Your project design may have to account for risks of lower probability during the life of the project result; such as earthquakes or extreme weather; but that is not the topic of project risk assessment. Exceptions may include insurance for events such as extreme weather (e.g., hurricane, and flood) on a construction project.

Risk Impact

Qualify or quantify risk impact in terms of the overall project schedule and cost; or of the expected return on investment for the project. LPM provides a unique measure of classifying the risk impact in terms of the project buffers for time and cost. The buffer size is an indicator of the common cause risk in the project; and therefore a reasonable basis to measure special-cause variation.

High impact. Anything that could cause an impact in excess of the project buffer on schedule, in excess of the cost buffer on cost, or otherwise result in client or project team dissatisfaction.

Moderate impact. An impact that would consume about two thirds of your project buffers, or all of your feeding buffers, but at least one third of the respective buffers.

Low impact. Consequences would not exceed one third of your project schedule or cost buffers.

Take Action!

The purpose of risk management is to identify and guide actions to reduce the potential impact of risks on your projects. You must take action to achieve the result. Performing a risk assessment has no value if you do not take action.

Monitor. You should plan monitor for the risks you elect to keep in your risk management list. Review the list with your team members at pre-planned intervals in your project meetings (e.g. once a week or month), and ask if any of the risk triggers seem to be immanent, if risks are past, or if new risks are perceived. Sometimes, you may need more formal monitoring for the risk triggers.

Prevent. Risk prevention activities you have elected to implement become part of your project plan. All you have to do to ensure that they are in place is to follow through on your project measurement and control process.

Prepare. Prepare for risk mitigation as part of your project plan. Include routine activities necessary to ensure the operability of your risk mitigation plans, such as fire inspections or emergency drills, as part of your project monitoring and control process.

You are now ready to move on to the next chapter and the product of all of your planning efforts: the project plan.

Summary of the Sixth Principle

- ❏ Risk management is the tool to manage special-cause variation.

- ❏ Risk management requires several steps, and at least the following:

    - o Identification.

    - o Analysis.

    - o Monitoring.

    - o Control.

- ❏ You must take action for your risk management to work!

Discussion Questions.

1. What have been some of the things that have occurred on projects you have worked on or know about?

2. How might the risks have been prevented?

3. How might the consequences of the risks have been limited?

References

Hilson, D. (2004). *When is a risk not a risk? (part 2)*. Retrieved Dec. 09, 2005, from Risk Doctor Web site: http://www.risk-doctor.com/pdf-briefings/risk-doctor07e.pdf June 22.

PMI. (2004). *A Guide to the Project Management Body of Knowledge, Third Edition*. Newtown Square, PA: Project Management Institute

Pritchard, C. (2001). *Risk Management: Concepts and Guidance*. Arlington, VA: ESI International

Wideman, R. (1992). *Project and Program RISK MANAGEMENT, A Guide to Managing Project Risk and Opportunities.* Newtown Square, PA: PMI

I keep six honest serving men,
(They taught me all I know);
Their names are What and Why and When
And How and Where and Who.

Rudyard Kipling

PRINCIPLE SEVEN: PROJECT PLAN

The Project Plan provides all project stakeholders the roadmap for project success. It provides both the project description and processes to achieve the project result. The project schedule and control to it are key elements of the Project Plan, and rely on an effective resource loaded and leveled project task network and critical chain plan. Projects must be pipelined through a bottleneck drum resource to establish when they should start and complete. All projects require necessary and sufficient project execution procedures, including at least project communication and change control processes.

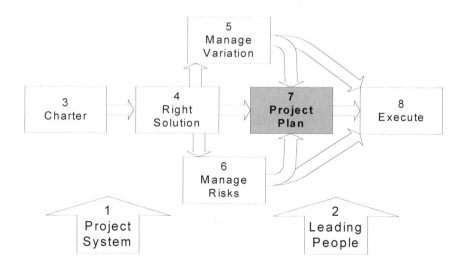

This principle focuses on creating and using an effective Project Plan (sometimes called a Project Execution Plan or Project Management Plan) to guide your project. It describes the content and process for deploying effective Project Plans.

A Project Plan is the primary tool to guide your project to success. While the form and content of Project Plans varies widely depending on the needs of your project and system, certain essentials are necessary for all project plans. Although we have included in this chapter the essentials leading up to a good project schedule, do not mistake a project schedule for a Project Plan. Although a project schedule is an essential part of your Project Plan, it is only part. This chapter starts by identifying the complete content you may need, and ends with helping you scale your specific Project Plan to the needs of your project.

A unique addition of multi-project Lean Project Management is the need to pipeline your project to ensure the flow of all projects in your system.

My experience with many dozens of projects supports the assertion that projects that effectively use a Project Plan succeed, while those that do not often fail and generally run into problems. The Project Management Institute's (PMI) Project Management Body of Knowledge (PMBOK Guide™,

2004) describes the content of a Project Plan, but somehow it is often overlooked as essential to success, while many of the other things in the PMBOK Guide are less essential, or not needed at all for some projects.

As with all LPM processes, you should scale the project plan to your projects and environment. Be cautious: despite the fact that an effective plan is the single most important waste prevention tool, people usually under-plan, and rarely over-plan.

Project Plan Content

PMI (p. 88) describes the Project Management Plan as defining, *"how the project is executed, monitored and controlled, and closed"*. You use it to:

- Guide project execution,

- Document project planning assumptions,

- Document project planning decisions,

- Facilitate communication among stakeholders,

- Define key management reviews, and

- Provide a baseline for project measurement and control.

You should scale the contents of a Project Plan to the scope of the project and other factors, but certain key elements are always necessary in one form or another. First, know that *a Project Plan is much more than a project schedule*. It includes everything the project stakeholders need to know to succeed on the project. Gray (p .76) uses the metaphor of the project manager as an orchestra conductor. If so, the Project Plan provides the music score.

Necessary elements include a clear statement of what the project is going to deliver (the Statement of Work, or SOW), responsibility assignment to deliver the SOW, and usually some estimate of cost and schedule. I like to use a fragment from a poem by Rudyard Kipling (at the start of this chapter) to keep focus on the necessary element of any plan. This little fragment captures the essence of Project Plans. Total Quality Management (TQM) terminology refers to these as "Five Ws and an H."

Figure 7-1 illustrates the two broad breakdowns of the necessary content of a Project Plan. It must define both the product (baseline) and the process. Product definition includes the scope of work, budget, and schedule for the project. Process definition includes all of the processes necessary to execute the project. People most often leave out or assume the latter part.

Figure 7-1: The Comprehensive Project Plan Integrates All Parts of a Project

While teaching seminars to a broad range of Project Managers, I have acquired informal survey results as to why it is difficult for many project managers to create a Project Plan that fulfils these functions. The most common theme is that they are judged based on actions accomplished (not necessarily the same as getting the project done right or quickest), and that most management sees planning as a waste of time, and often as unnecessary overhead. This is unfortunate (for them), as studies demonstrate each dollar invested in planning saves over $1,000 in the final project result through reduced cost, accelerated schedule, reduced quality problems or some combination. You may wish to browse the PMI WEB site for additional information on this. The Construction Industry Institute (CII) and the Software Engineering Institute (SEI) are additional sources for the kinds of specialty projects they represent. All provide data to support the project delivery improvement that results from effective Project Plans.

Project Plan Process

Project Plan development requires an iterative process. Figure 7-2 illustrates the general flow of the process as a waterfall type of process. The figure fails to show the many times most Project Plans have to recycle all the way back to the Work Breakdown Structure (WBS) to ensure an integrated plan. You can and often will branch back from each step in the process to a previous step or steps, as the process of what PMI calls 'progressive elaboration' takes place.

Note that there is only one block for Project Control Processes. Do not be deceived by this: the PMI (p. 89) lists 15 potential subsidiary control plans as "not limited to". As a minimum, you need a process to control the project scope, schedule, and cost if it is important to your project (believe it or not, cost is not a significant consideration in many projects). Controlling these elements requires an effective formal project change control process. Do not leave home without one! All project managers that complain about *scope creep* admit to having an ineffective project change control process.

Project Task Network

The task network models how your project will perform. It will lead to the schedule for your project, and often helps develop the project budget as well. You will use the network throughout your project to authorize and control work, and to report progress on your project. Purposes of the project task network include:

❑ Define project delivery date.

❑ Determine sequence of activities necessary to create all project deliverables.

❑ Estimate project resources.

❑ Enable resource scheduling.

❑ Schedule material delivery.

❑ Determine material order schedules.

❑ Provide the baseline for project performance measurement.

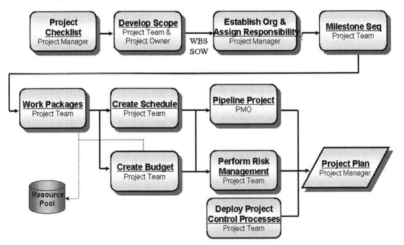

Figure 7-2: Project Plan Process Develops All Parts of a Project Plan

You will use scheduling software to build, status, and report on your project. Over the last twenty years, microcomputer project software has incorporated a bewildering array of features. Nearly anyone can learn how to point and click to activate many (if not all) of these features. That does not make you an effective scheduler.

Working as a trainer and consultant, I get to review project schedules for many organizations and many types of projects. *Most* demonstrate very poor basic scheduling expertise. Some of these schedulers spend extensive time using software features they should not be using, defeating the elements of the tool that they should be using.

Even the simplest scheduling software today exhibits capability far beyond that which I started with in the late 1960s. We successfully ran many large projects with that much simpler software. You can run successful projects with nearly any schedule software, and for smaller projects, even none at all. Software is not going to make your project successful. Concentrate on the basics of building and using your project network, and you will have a successful project.

Network Building

The task network defines all of the tasks in your project necessary to produce all of the project deliverables. Network building is a team sport. The more you can engage the task managers and resources that will perform the work in the network building, the greater the chances are of having an effective network. When you bring the team together to build the network, you should already have:

❑ The project Vision.

❑ The project WBS, including responsibility assignment.

❑ The key Milestone sequence chart.

❑ Overall project planning assumptions.

❏ The project issue/action list.

You should set up your planning space with flip charts to capture:

❏ Work package assumptions.

❏ Risks.

❏ New issues and actions.

You develop the task network by starting with each deliverable on your WBS, and working backwards asking the question, "What inputs do I need for this deliverable?" The backwards planning approach can be a powerful tool, similar to designing the kanban process for work pull in Lean manufacturing. The kanban process is a simple way to move work through a production system by passing kanban cards "upstream" (or backwards) through the production process, to pull the work along as needed by the downstream (successor) task. Backwards planning can help you take this perspective on project work.

You create a task (which should be a verb-noun pair) to produce each input. Task relationships or links tie the output of one task to the input of another task.

You may use a variety of tools to create your task network. The all-time favorite is a flip-chart easel and a supply of yellow sticky notes. You start with a deliverable from your WBS, and work backwards until you have something that you must create directly from the project scope statement. You are linking the outputs of tasks to provide the necessary input of successor tasks.

One significant limitation using the computer to input your tasks is that it encourages forward planning and linking the tasks, vs. the backwards development suggested above. Some people prefer one way to the other. Use whatever works for your team.

166

If you choose to build your network directly on the computer, using a projector (a viable option), or when you decide to input the tasks to the computer, you should set scheduling options before proceeding. Figure 7-3 illustrates the MS Project™ schedule options tab. This is the way I set it up.

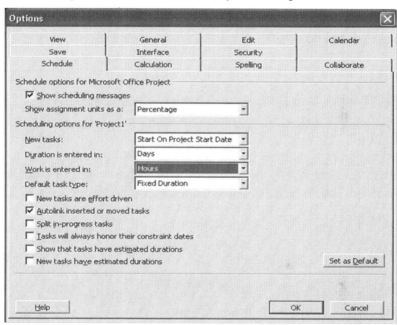

Figure 7-3: Set your schedule options before entering the schedule into your schedule tool

You should set your task type to fixed duration. Other choices can interfere with the program's ability to identify a critical chain. When making changes to schedules, you may need to highlight all of the tasks, and reset the constraint for all tasks back to *As soon as possible*, before you recalculate the critical chain.

NOTE: The task constraint appears on the Advanced tab of the task information window. You can change the constraint for many tasks at once by highlighting all of the tasks, and then bringing up the task window.

Microsoft Project™ also includes, by default, an item called *Effort Driven Scheduling*. This feature uses the work equation to adjust your task duration. Although a noble intent, in some ways, it causes unpredictable changes in your task duration estimates. Most people find this annoying, and it can complicate critical chain procedures. Be sure to turn it off as your default, and set your default task type to fixed duration. Turn off task splitting.

The Gantt Chart

You will usually enter your tasks into schedule software using the Gantt chart view. Figure 7-4 illustrates the MS Project Gantt chart. Note that I have added a column to display the WBS number, which MS Project will enter for you as you enter tasks, and a Contact column. Note also that I do not display task date columns. Task dates are meaningless.

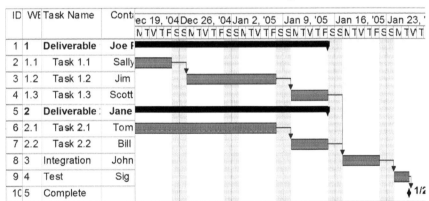

ID	WE	Task Name	Cont:
1	1	**Deliverable**	**Joe**
2	1.1	Task 1.1	Sally
3	1.2	Task 1.2	Jim
4	1.3	Task 1.3	Scott
5	2	**Deliverable**	**Jane**
6	2.1	Task 2.1	Tom
7	2.2	Task 2.2	Bill
8	3	Integration	John
9	4	Test	Sig
1C	5	Complete	

Figure 7-4: The Gantt chart shows the task timeline. Most current versions also show task relationships.

MS Project provides a number of other pre-defined columns, and allows you to define columns to present other information. The one additional column I use frequently is labeled Contact. You can put the Work Package and Task Manager's names in that field.

168

This is the procedure you can use to enter tasks in MS Project:

1. Enter a deliverable name.

2. Enter the tasks under the deliverable, in the general order that they are related.

3. Highlight the tasks under the deliverable, and use the arrow on the menu to indent the tasks under the deliverable. This makes the deliverable a summary task, as illustrated above by Deliverable 1 and 2.

4. Highlight the tasks that link in a top down chain, and click on the chain icon on the menu to link them.

5. Add other links to other tasks. You can do this several ways in MS Project.

6. Go back to the top task, and enter the mean task duration and resources. (Note: entering a task duration of zero sets the task type to a Milestone.)

7. Index down and repeat step 6 for each task.

You can either enter all of the deliverables first, or enter them as you go, keeping track to assure that you are following the WBS.

The MS Project Task Entry view provides a split screen for task entry. It shows the Gantt chart above, and (by default) task resources and predecessors in the lower half of the screen (Figure 7-5). You can change the view in the lower half by right clicking in the lower half of the screen, and select other alternatives, including task notes. I sometimes choose the task notes view, and use it for the Basis of Estimate (BOE), but you may use the task notes for other purposes, including keeping support resource notes and/or task status notes. Your project plan should specify how you want people to use this field.

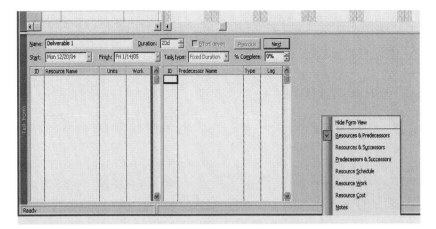

Figure 7-5: The lower half of the split screen in the MS Project Task Entry view, showing the options available by right clicking.

Resources. Once you are satisfied with the task network, you need to identify the resources necessary to perform each task. This is called resource loading the task network. LPM plans should always have a resource for a task. The resource can be the same as the Task Manager, but need not be, and usually are not on larger projects. On larger projects, the Task Manager frequently also serves as supervisor or work leader. If you have only one resource, assign 100% of that resource to the task and estimate the duration accordingly. If you use more than one resource on the task, at least one resource should be at 100%: the resource that determines the task duration.

You should always put as many resources on a task as you can provide to perform the task effectively. For some tasks, that might be one person. For others, it might be many people. You should NOT arbitrarily assign a fraction of the organization's resources to a given project, nor should you assign the resources that determine the task duration to spend a fraction of their time on various projects. It is fine to assign resources to tasks on multiple projects: the LPM relay racer rule requires that resources accomplish this by completing the task on one project, and then move on to the next task, which may be on another project, rather than attempting to progress multiple tasks in parallel, which LPM calls bad multitasking.

For larger organizations and projects, it is generally best to identify resources by skill type initially, rather than by name. The reason is that this gives you maximum flexibility when the task comes up for work to assign an available person. This can help the flow of your projects. Of course, if there is only one technical person in the company qualified to do the task, by all means identify the resource by that name.

You may have multiple numbers of resources on a task (e.g. 5 Engineers, or 500%). You may also have multiple types of resources on a task. Support resources may be required at less than 100% of the task. You should set a lower limit; e.g. 10%, and not include resources that would be required at less than that percentage.

You need a way to alert part-time task resources when a task is likely to need them, and to help them prioritize which task to work on next. These resources may only be needed for a short time during the overall task duration. If you put in their work hours, the task will only require a fraction of a person over the duration of the task. If you have many of these tasks in a network, and then resource level the network, computer resource leveling may move these tasks around to level the support resources: this could be the tail wagging the dog.

For example, a physical job on heavy equipment may require riggers to remove the equipment after disconnecting it, and to put it back into place near the end of a repair task. You could put these activities in as separate activities, but on larger projects going to that level of detail might explode the network into many tens of thousands of activities. The final solution to this depends on many factors, so I cannot generalize it here. You need a process to engage part-time resources properly on these types of tasks.

Part-time resources often show up in tasks to review work product; e.g. five different people must review a major document. Unless you provide a separate task for this document review, most computer programs will spread the review hours across the whole task duration. Even if you use a separate review task, resource leveling will frequently move the review task so it does not interfere with any other tasks of all the reviewers, because the reviewers are scheduled 100% on their other work tasks. Thus, you may find the review of a completed piece of work far removed in the schedule from the actual work completion. Most people do not like this result, and some blame the schedule network or software as being faulty. The schedule network and software are not faulty; the software did exactly what it is designed to do. The problem lies in how the scheduler identified the resources. As with support resources, you need to come up with an effective way to plan review tasks. I usually do not resource load them if they demand only a few hours of a given resource time; but add in the task notes a list of required reviewers.

Task duration estimate. The duration estimate should be a "50/50" estimate. That is, if the average resource of the type assigned were to do that task many times over, half of the times it should take longer than the estimated duration, and half the time it should take less than the estimated duration.

When making the switch to LPM, people usually do not have a good idea of what a 50/50, relay racer task duration might be. Studies have shown that if asked, people with similar experience will tend to give approximately the same duration estimate for a 90/10 estimate as they would give for a 50/50 estimate. Available data suggests that in most cases, the 50/50 estimate should be half or less than the 90/10 estimate. If it is an organization that has been engaged in bad multitasking (most organizations, in my experience), the 50/50 estimate should be much less than one-half of the 90/10 estimate.

For this reason, the common practice when first starting with LPM is to ask people to estimate as they normally do, and then put one-half of that duration estimate into the task duration in the schedule. Buffer(s) at the end of the chains of tasks absorb the other half of the task duration.

There are exceptions where task duration is not driven by resource work, for example a five-day burn-in test. In those cases, you should set the duration as necessary.

Relationships. Most project planning tools provide for a variety of relationships between tasks. Dependencies usually include:

❑ Finish to start.

❑ Start to start.

❑ Finish to finish.

❑ Start to finish.

Most project scheduling tools allow you to place leads and lags between tasks. A lead-time is a negative lag. Generally, it is just best to use finish to start relationships. This avoids much planning ambiguity.

MS Project uses the finish to start relationship, with zero lag, as the default. Some critical chain software only allows the use of the finish to start task relationship. If necessary, you can reproduce the effect of all of the other relationships, including lags, using finish to start relationships and dummy tasks. I do not encourage this.

Constraints. Most project planning tools provide for a plethora of constraints that you can place on tasks. They may include:

❑ Start no earlier than (SNET).

❑ Start no later than.

❑ Must start on.

❑ Must finish on.

❑ Finish no earlier than.

❑ Finish no later than.

❑ As soon as possible.

❑ As late a possible.

Whenever possible, you should use the *As soon as possible* constraint when entering tasks. This is the MS Project default. Some critical chain software will not allow using some or all of the other constraints. The reason you should not use fixed date constraints is that they can adversely influence identifying the critical chain.

When applying critical chain, the scheduling software will move your tasks. First, the software will move them when it resource levels to find the critical chain. Then, it may move them to fit in the feeding buffers, while maintaining resource leveling. The last step for a single project will move tasks to start chains of tasks as late as possible. Finally, pipelining of projects can move the start dates of entire projects. Thus, applying other constraints can have unexpected and undesired impacts on this process.

Resource leveling. LPM requires that you resource level your network before identifying the critical chain. Resource leveling moves tasks so that, for any time interval, the total resource demanded by all of the tasks scheduled in that interval do not exceed the number of resources available. For this to work, you have to specify the number of resources available of each type of resource. In MS Project, you do this on the resource sheet.

Resource leveling delays tasks as necessary to match supply and demand. The trick is deciding which tasks to delay, so that the project completes in the shortest possible time. Scheduling software provides various algorithms for doing this, and allows the users certain choices on how those algorithms are applied. For the mathematically inclined, it might interest you to note that the resource-leveling problem is what is called in mathematics as an *np-hard* problem: you cannot prove an optimum solution for such a problem. Therefore, the resource leveling algorithms seek to provide a good answer. Most schedule software allows optional resource leveling approaches.

Figure 7-6 illustrates the resource leveling options I usually select when using MS Project. Note that the leveling order can affect how MS Project delays tasks to level resources. This choice can also affect the choice of critical chain. If there are certain tasks you want to stay early in the project, e.g. tasks that reduce project risks, you can use task priority and select the leveling order "Priority, Standard" in the leveling order box on figure 7-6 to keep the higher priority tasks earlier in the project plan. You must also then set high priority on those tasks, using the task dialog box. Some critical chain software does not allow you control over those options, but one mentioned earlier (CCPM+) does.

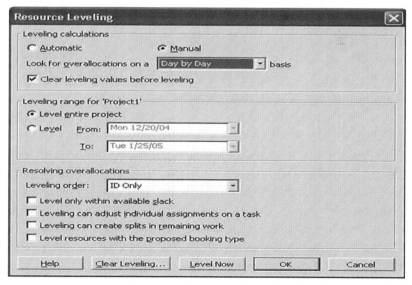

Figure 7-6: Recommended options for resource leveling.

Many project managers criticize the resource leveling algorithms, because they sometimes yield results that do not match the project manager's intuition. I have always found that when this concern exists, the project manager or scheduler does not understand how resource leveling works. Resource leveling is a digital computer operation performed with an algorithm. That algorithm does exactly what you tell it to do. The algorithm does not have insight into task content. If you do not like the results, you need to change the input to get a different output.

You should not get overly concerned about the task sequences that emerge from resource leveling. Your understanding of variation should assure you that the project is not going to play out like those seemingly solid bars on your Gantt chart: every task is going to take less or more time than the amount of time shown. The operation of resource leveling provides you some assurance that the overall time allocated for the project is resource feasible; you should not interpret it as meaning you must do a task placed before another task for resource leveling purposes to represent the actual sequence to perform those tasks. LPM provides dynamic information to answer, for each resource, *"Which task should I work on next?"* That answer depends on the progress of predecessor tasks, both in the technical chain and for that resource.

The PERT Chart

One type of task network diagram, frequently called a *PERT Chart* illustrates the tasks and certain information about them, but often does not include dates for the tasks. The PERT chart is a good visual illustration of a task network. Figure 7-7 illustrates a portion of a task network. Each task has an identified WBS number, a name, and other information. If you can, you should suppress task date information on LPM projects, because task dates are meaningless.

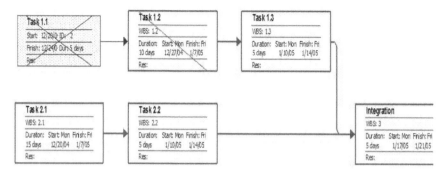

Figure 7-7: PERT chart provides an illustration of the task network.

Sometimes the PERT chart provides a useful way to display a complex project on a large format print out. It is sometimes easier to check all the predecessor/successor links using the PERT chart. The MS Project PERT chart will also illustrate progress to a degree, placing a single angled line through a started task, and a double line across a completed task.

PERT stands for Program Evaluation and Review Technique. Applying the name to the chart is something of a misnomer, but it represents common practice. PERT includes a method of probabilistic planning, using three estimates for each task duration or cost. Although there are some weaknesses with this approach as initially applied, you could use it to estimate buffers as you mature your LPM approach, and if you do not wish to go to the ultimate step of using Monte-Carlo simulation (i.e. a statistical model) to size buffers.

Stuff to generally not waste time on. Many scheduling tools come with a bewildering array of features. Many of the features control things that are in the noise level of your project plan; i.e. well less than the stochastic variation of the task duration and time estimates. You are better off not wasting your time on them. One example is the ability to put in calendars for specific resources or even for specific tasks. I am sure that there are projects that really needed (or thought they

177

did) each of those features, but my experience is that most of them waste time and cause potential errors downstream when things change.

Network Building Good Practices

The following good practices will help you create effective task networks.

- ❏ Keep the number of tasks to the minimum necessary to create deliverables.

- ❏ Assure that the number of tasks are sufficient to guide task manager handoffs.

- ❏ Tasks should enable objective completion measurement---identifiable output.

- ❏ The critical chain should have at least ten activities, but more (at least 20) is better.

- ❏ No single task should consume more than 10% of the critical chain.

- ❏ Tasks should not go beyond about one month in duration. (There may be exceptions, of course.)

- ❏ Review your network for non-value adding work, and eliminate it.

- ❏ Review your network to reduce the seven causes of waste.

The following are some common mistakes I see in task networks. You should try to avid making them, and consider them when you review a network.

- ❏ Unlinked tasks (aka loose ends): all paths of tasks must lead to a single ending milestone.

- ❏ Unnecessary date constraints (contractual milestones).

- ❏ Tasks without identifiable outputs.

- ❏ Task durations based on multitasking.
- ❏ Faulty logic.
- ❏ Links to or from summary tasks (confuses the software on finding the critical chain.)
- ❏ Items on the critical chain that are not critical, e.g. documentation.
- ❏ Extra links.
- ❏ Project deliverables not identified in WBS.
- ❏ Excessively long tasks without measurable performance.
- ❏ Too few tasks on the critical chain.
- ❏ Too many parallel paths.

You may want to use the above as a checklist to review your completed network.

Finding the Critical Chain

The next step in a LPM is to identify the constraint of the single project: the critical chain. The critical chain is the longest path through the project after resource leveling. The critical chain can jump project logic paths, but only when the tasks it is jumping on share the same critical resource. The best way to identify the critical chain is work backwards through the resource leveled critical path network, identifying the critical chain tasks as you go. You can cause most scheduling programs to display the resource along with the task, to help you perform this function if you are doing it manually. However, if you have more than a few dozen tasks, or if your tasks use multiple resources, it quickly becomes very difficult to identify the critical chain manually. You need scheduling software to help you do it.

Figure 7-8 shows an example critical path schedule (Dark bars). The figure illustrates the resource loading for each task. The resource loading is 100% unless shown otherwise. Note that Fred is overloaded for the second and part of the third week of the project, and that Elaine is overloaded for part of the fourth week of the project. The project would be very unlikely to finish before 1/25. If we were to resource level this plan, the projected finish date would move out two and a half weeks.

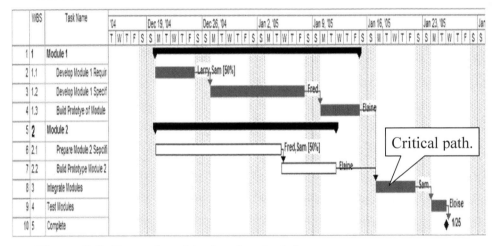

Figure 7-8: Example critical path schedule.

The next steps in creating a critical chain project are to put in the 50/50 duration estimates and to resource level the plan. Then you are able to identify the critical chain. Figure 7-9 illustrates the network after resource leveling and reducing the task durations. Note that the resource leveling moved task 2.1 to follow task 1.2, in order to level out Fred. Doing that also eliminated Elaine's overload. The critical path becomes undefined after resource leveling, as the longest path through the project does not track through the predecessor/successor task relationships. Different software would identify the critical path differently for this network.

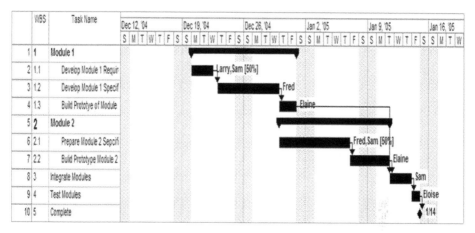

Figure 7-9: Resource-leveled network with 50/50 task durations.

Figure 7-10 presents the critical chain for the example project. Note that the critical chain is not the same set of tasks that comprised the critical path. The critical chain jumps logic paths on resource Fred. Task 1.3 (WBS code) was on the critical path, but is not on the critical chain. Tasks 2.1 and 2.2 were not on the critical path, but are on the critical chain. The software's resource leveling moved task 2.1 (WBS Code) to follow task 1.2, thus placing it on the critical chain.

Figure 7-10: Critical chain for the example project.

Some might suggest we could have made a shorter plan by having Fred do some work on task 2.1 before the input was ready for task 1.2, and then move to task 1.2, complete it, and move to task 2.1. Fred might actually do that in project execution, but for planning purposes, the above sequence is better, as it avoids leaving a partially completed task. Task switching always causes some loss of efficiency, and often introduces errors. Furthermore, if Fred is available prior to the input for task 1.2, he might be able to spend valuable time doing pre-work for task 1.2, or perhaps even for both tasks 1.2 and 2.1, for example getting the specifications 'boiler plate' and common material ready for the other input. Since task 1.2 is on the critical chain, doing pre-work to accelerate it will accelerate project completion.

The final step to create a single project LPM plan is to size and insert buffers. Figure 7-11 illustrates the sample project LPM plan. This plan has one Feeding Buffer and one Project Buffer. All projects will have only one Project Buffer, but most projects will contain many Feeding Buffers. In this case, the completed critical chain plan is a little longer than the initial critical path plan, but significantly shorter than what we would have obtained by simply resource leveling the critical path plan.

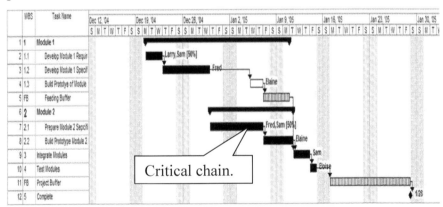

Figure 7-11: Critical chain project plan with buffers.

For larger projects, the initial critical chain you come up with is usually not right!

- ❑ It is usually too long.

- ❑ It frequently contains activities that should not be holding back your project.

Therefore, you should carefully examine the initial network, and revise as needed to get to a workable plan. Some of the steps you can take are as follows:

- ❑ Use multiple cycles of Identify->Exploit-> Subordinate

  - o Verify the task logic.

  - o Check if there are gaps in the critical chain. Can you remove the cause?

  - o Do you have any task constraints that are stretching out the critical chain?

  - o Can tasks be done in parallel?

  - o Does one task have to finish completely before another can start?

- ❑ Consider revising resource assignments:

  - o Can you use additional resources on critical chain tasks to reduce duration and make them go off the critical chain (another task becomes longer duration)?

  - o Can you apply different resources to perform the task, changing the resource driven path?

Once you are satisfied with the network and critical chain, you will need to size and place buffers to complete your single project plan. The next section covers pipelining multiple projects.

Pipelining

The final step in setting the schedules for LPM projects in most organizations is to pipeline the projects. Pipelining establishes project pull by setting the start and finish dates for all projects in the pipeline. Pipelining is the necessary last step in any organization that performs multiple projects. It enables greatly accelerated project performance. Pipelining delays the start of whole projects, thereby enabling all projects to finish sooner. It prevents overloading the organizational resources with a capacity constraint buffer. It is the project level equivalent of resource leveling, but has a different effect than simply resource-leveling multiple projects.

I like to use an example that I first heard presented by Karl Buckridge, of Critical Chain, Ltd. in the U.K. I have embellished his rendition a little, but hopefully kept his key point. Think of yourself as the dock-master (resource manager) with a staff of five who unload ships for you. One Monday morning, five ships (projects) show up at your dock, and the captains (project managers) are all clamoring to have their ship unloaded. Each ship requires five person-days of work to unload. To keep all the captains happy, you assign one person to each ship, and on Friday evening, all five ships are ready to go back to sea for another load. That is an example of bad multitasking at the group level, and is the way many resource managers seek to satisfy all of their customers.

If, however, you wanted to maximize throughput of the ships, you could take another approach. If you put all five of your people on one ship on Monday, they will complete the five person-days of unloading work on Monday evening, saving 4 days or 80% on unloading (project) duration. Then you put everyone on the second ship, and it finishes Tuesday evening, saving 60% on duration. Similarly, by pipelining the other ships, ship three finishes on Wednesday, saving 40%, ship four on Thursday, saving 20%, and ship five on Friday. You do not save time on ship five this time around, but you do save time on all the other projects (up to 80%), with no additional work.

Further, once you have started pipelining ships this way (i.e. stopped the multitasking at the group level), each ship will in the future come back in rotation, and on average have no delay: in other words, you will accelerate them all by 80%. The actual result will probably be somewhat less because the actual rotation will have variation and queuing, but you see how this alternate approach can easily save half the duration, on average.

Refer back to the pipelining discussion in principle one, and figure 1-11 on how to work pipelining. If you do not have the software to automate pipelining, you can do it by generating, on the same time scale, resource loading charts for the drum resource, and determining how much you have to delay one project relative to another so as to maintain, on average, the capacity constraint buffer protective capacity. You should generally put the *big rocks* in first, as table1-2 suggests.

The initial discussions about pipelining suggested you had to prioritize projects for sequencing in the pipeline. This sometimes causes a blocking point for management teams, as everyone wants to think their project is most important, and most management (despite the best efforts of Stephen Covey) has a scarcity mentality: if you win (i.e. have a higher priority than me), then I must lose. The point is to *accelerate all projects* by pipelining, so the common (mis)understanding does not apply: pipelining creates a win-win for all projects. If your organization maturity requires that you avoid using the word priority, do not use it. You can use words like sequence number or pipeline number, or whatever you like (a rose by any other name...). The point is to come out of the pipelining process with project start dates that maximize *organization* throughput.

Pipelining does **NOT** seek to level all resources across all projects, and thus has a radically different result than any non LPM approach to planning multiple projects. Leveling all resources across all projects would stretch out the duration of all projects. It would also require all project schedules to change as new projects are added to the pipeline. Not leveling all resources maximizes project throughput.

The pipelining process uses a resource type shared across the multiple projects, called the drum resource, to delay project starts. The drum resource should be the resource thought to have the highest demanded load to capacity ratio (utilization), and should have relatively long task durations. Pipelining moves whole projects until the drum resource loading is leveled, on average. Figure 7-12 illustrates an example of drum resource loading demand for four projects, with all starting in week one.

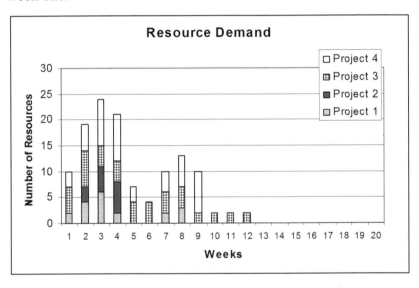

Figure 7-12: Example drum loading chart for multiple projects before sequencing. Each bar color/design represents a different project.

Assuming 12 available resources, figure 7-13 shows one viable pipelining solution, achieved by delaying the start of project 2 by two weeks and project four by seven weeks.

Generally, the time bucket used for pipelining should be longer than the time bucket used to level resources within the individual project.

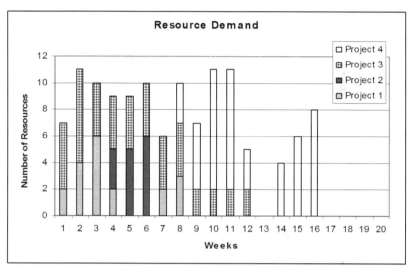

Figure 7-13: One viable sequencing solution with 12 available resources.

Pipelining should allow a *capacity constraint buffer* in the loading of the drum resource. The capacity constraint buffer plans the loading of the drum resource at less than its full capacity. The reason to do this is to avoid excessive delays waiting for the drum resource to be able to work on tasks. The effective capacity constraint buffer for the first 12 weeks of the example shown in figures 7-12 and 13 is 25 %. You might be tempted to start project 4 a week earlier, but then the capacity constraint buffer for the first ten weeks would be only 20%, indicating a growing possibility of delay. Of course, you could *actually start* project 4 early if the resources are available, even if you plan the seven-week delay.

Pipelining can lead to apparent temporary overloading of other than the drum resource when initially sequencing the projects. This is fine, because the overall duration of the projects, including the buffers, will allow all resources to complete their required work within the overall duration. The LPM project execution approach provides the tools to manage this. Since the drum resource is the resource with the highest demanded load to capacity ratio, and it is leveled, the demand to capacity for all other resources will be lower than that for the drum resource.

Cost Estimate

At the proposal and project Charter stage, you usually must develop the Total Cost of Ownership (TCO) for the proposed solution. The TCO includes the development, implementation, and ongoing maintenance costs for the proposed solution. Compare the (risk adjusted) projected benefits for the project to the project TCO to estimate the Return on Investment (ROI).

Bottom-up estimating is the most accurate way to create both schedule and cost estimates. Figure 4-6 illustrated the essential features of a WBS. You should limit your WBS to three levels like the illustration, but you will have entirely different deliverables. PMI's *Practice Standard for Work Breakdown Structures* provides a wide variety of WBS examples for you to use to gain insight.

Parametric tools are available for preliminary development estimates because the project cost estimate can usually afford to have greater variation. COCOMO (Royce, 1998, pp. 265-281), a famous model for parametric estimating of software projects, provides a top-down cost estimate using equations of the following form:

$$\text{Effort} = C1 \ EAF \ (\text{Size})^{P1}$$
$$\text{Time} = C2 \ (\text{Effort})^{P2}$$

Where:

> Effort = number of staff months
>
> C1, C2 = scaling coefficients
>
> EAF = Effort Adjustment factor that characterizes the

domain

> Size = Size of end product measured by the number of delivered source instructions
>
> P1, P2 = Exponents

Such parametric approaches are generally not as accurate as bottom-up estimating, but are useful at the project selection stage and provide a general validation of a bottom-up estimate. You can find substantial information on this model on the Internet.

You should estimate each task in your plan at its mean value, with an indication of the uncertainty of that value; e.g. $1,000\pm150$ person-hours. For each cost estimate, give your Basis of Estimate (BOE). For example, 'Similar development on project X took 500 hours, but this project is about twice as complex.' Alternatively, "Vendor quote from XYZ Corp. on March 15, 2003." An Excel spreadsheet is appropriate for your cost estimate.

Cost estimates are uncertain. Can you predict what the price of regular gas will be in Boise, Idaho next July? Indeed, there is no single price today. Larger variations exist for many project elements. Statistical tools are the only effective way to handle such variation. We will cover how to use such tools simply later on.

Project Procedures

The list of *potential* project control processes and procedures can be long, but should *consider* at least some of the following:

- Communication
- Human Resources/Training

- Requirements Management

- Quality (Including Product Acceptance)

- Configuration Management/ Document Control

- Security

- Safety

- Privacy

- Project Closeout

You should be sure that your control processes do not introduce non-value adding work or waste. Although with knowledge work it can make it more difficult to implement the Lean approach to direct visual control through management by sight (Ohno, p. 129), you should seek to design your systems to provide this feature.

Project risk management has become a leading topic in project literature in recent years. I believe this is due in part to some misconceptions about the nature of the uncertainty inherent in Project Plans (i.e. misunderstanding progressive elaboration and variation). However, it is important to consider what might go wrong with your project, and take the necessary steps to prevent or mitigate events that you can foresee. The previous section described the risk management process, and your Project Plan is the place to document it.

Table 7-1 illustrates a simple matrix for a communication plan. Your communication plan may be somewhat simpler than this, or much more complex, depending on the project. For example, public environmental clean-up projects require formal communication plans that may run to many hundreds of pages.

Table 7-1: Sample communication plan for a modest size project conveys necessary information.

Stakeholder	Information Need	Frequency	Medium	Response
Project Owner (Customer) Executive	• High level scope, schedule, cost performance • Problems and proposed actions • Required actions by customer	Monthly	WEB site, Presentations, Report	Required in 3 working days
Project Team	• Detailed task plan • Detailed task status	Weekly	Meetings, Meeting Minutes, WEB site, Email	Required in 1 working day
Project Manager's Supervision	• Detailed cost, schedule, quality performance • Problems, proposed actions, assistance required	Weekly	Report Status and Review Meetings	Required in 5 working days
Project Resource Suppliers	• Detailed resource requirements • Performance feedback	Weekly	Report, Information Meetings	Required in 3 working days
Project Result Users	• Required actions by users • Plans for user involvement	Weekly	Report, Information Meetings	Required in 3 working days
Involved Organization Management	• Coordination information; What/When	Monthly or Weekly	Report, Published Meeting Minutes	Required in 5 working days

Perhaps the most common and troublesome project communication tool is the project meeting. Successful project leaders always ensure effective project meetings through following the simple rules (very often overlooked) for meetings:

1. Make sure a meeting is necessary.

2. Make sure all of the people that need to be there attend, and only those who need to be there. Publish an agenda before the meeting.

3. Clarify the agenda and meeting expectations at the start of the meeting.

4. Unless it is a meeting to resolve a particular issue, do not attempt to resolve all issues in the meeting. Take the issues down, and assign *a* person to lead the resolution of it.

5. Summarize the results of the meeting when done, and publish the results as meeting minutes to inform all who need to know the results.

Above all, keep meetings as short as possible.

Do not use meetings to determine the status of your project. You should status your project schedule before your weekly project meeting, and use the meeting to communicate decisions and assign actions as necessary to move the project forward.

All projects will have changes. Rigorous change management leads to effective projects and happy stakeholders. Figure 7-14 illustrates an example change control process. There are two key elements to effective change control processes:

1. They must operate rapidly to disposition changes. A backlog of unresolved changes is a sure sign of project disaster.

2. Change requests must include an estimate of the impacts on project critical success factors, at least including project scope, cost, and schedule. These estimates must assess the cumulative and interactive effect of multiple changes. The interactive effect can often be much larger than the actual change itself.

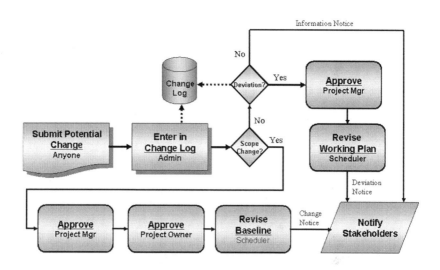

Figure 7-14: Example change control process illustrates key steps.

As I was preparing this write-up, an issue of PM Network (2005) arrived, with a failed project case as the lead article. The failed project had 2,500 change requests, and the project customer claimed that only 50 of them were actual changes. The article concludes that both parties were responsible for a failed scope management plan. They did not agree on what constituted a change, or on how to handle disputed requests. Large projects require a change control board, the leader of whom must keep the backlog of unresolved change requests to a minimal level; usually no more than a week or two of requests.

Grading Your Project Plan

Table 7-2 illustrates one way to grade the content of your project plans to the size and risk of your projects. You could use other criteria to decide, but the general trend should be towards more project plan content as projects become larger and have more risk.

Table 7-2: Grading the Project Plan

Project Size

	Small	Large
Low	**Simple Project Plan** -Charter -WBS (With Responsibility) -Budget (Spreadsheet) -Schedule (Resourced)	**Moderate** -Small Project Plan -WBS, Scope Statement, Work Packages -Integrated CSCS
High	**Moderate** -Small Project Plan -Design & Peer Review -Risk Management Plan -Quality Plan	**Full Project Plan** -All Project Plan Elements -Supporting Plans -Procedures -Process Training -Project Controls Function

(Left axis label: Project Risk — Low / High)

A small, low-risk project may only require a charter, a WBS (with responsibility assignment), a budget and a schedule. Internal projects may not even need a budget. At the other extreme, large and high risk projects may require extensive planning effort and documentation, including a number of stand-alone documents and procedures to support and implement the Project Plan.

In the case of the larger projects, I have found it a good idea to keep the project plan itself to a modest size (e.g. no more than 50 pages) for even the largest projects (i.e. several billion dollars). The reason is that no one will carry around or read a document larger than that. Most large projects now have document repositories on a computer server, and it is simple to hyperlink from inside the main project plan to all of the supporting information.

However you choose to configure your project plan, you must keep the update process fast and simple. You should keep track of the changes with a revision number, date, and explanation, and ensure to notify all project stakeholders when the plan is updated. Keeping the plan in electronic form greatly simplifies this process.

Summary of the Seventh Principle

Project Plans are a primary key to project success. You should ensure that all projects you lead have an effective Project Plan, with the content properly adjusted to the scope of the project and your project environment, and that everyone on your project uses the plan.

- ❑ A project plan is much more than a schedule.
- ❑ The project plan defines the project deliverables, schedule, and cost.
- ❑ The project task network is the key to effective execution.
    - ○ You must identify resource requirements, and level your network to ensure sufficient resource capacity.
    - ○ Assure the critical chain is critical.
    - ○ Exploit the critical chain.
    - ○ Subordinate to the critical chain.
- ❑ In a multi-project environment, pipelining establishes the project start and finish *dates*.

❑ The project plan defines all of the necessary and sufficient project control processes as simply as possible. As a minimum, all projects require a communication plan and change control process.

❑ You should grade the content of your project plans to the needs of the project. Smaller and less risky projects require less plan content than larger and higher risk projects.

Discussion Questions

1. Describe the Project Plans you have seen or participated in developing or using. What were their strengths? What were their weaknesses? Were there gaps? Was there excess information that was not useful?

2. How does your Project Plan process ensure that there is no non-value-adding work?

3. How does your Project Plan process ensure that you have eliminated the potential causes of waste?

4. Discuss how your company determines the expected financial (or other goal unit) benefits of projects, how they monitor this benefit, and what the success rate is.

5. How would you judge the quality of the project networks currently used by your organization, or on projects you have worked on?

6. Are the elements of network planning that would be difficult in your organization?

7. Do your projects have special considerations that would require specific network modeling approaches?

8. Do people currently multitask in your organization? How many tasks do people work on at one time?

9. Has your organization identified the drum resource? If not, what resource do you think it would be, and why?

References

Gray, C., Larson, E. (2001). *Project Management: The Managerial Process*. Boston: McGraw-Hill

Ohno, T. (1988). *Toyota Production System: Beyond Large-Scale Production*. Portland, OR: Productivity Press.

Project Management Institute. (2004). *A Guide to The Project Management Body of Knowledge, Third Edition*. Newtown Square, PA: Project Management Institute

Royce, W. (1998). *SOFTWARE PROJECT MANAGEMENT: A UNIFIED FRAMEWORK*. Reading, MA: Addison Wesley

Principle Eight: Executing

Whatever I might have (initially) thought,
Once I have started or undertaken (a task),
I will not think about anything else.
With my mind focused upon it,
I will pursue it for as long as it takes.

If one (acts) in this way, all projects will be done well.
Otherwise, neither (the earlier nor the latter) will be accomplished.

Santideva, ~800 AD

PRINCIPLE EIGHT: EXECUTING

Relay racer task performance underlies the final principle to Lean Project Management. The project leader enables relay racer task performance by helping task managers decide which task to work on. Task information informs the project team when and where to take action on the project to recover buffers. The most effective project leaders focus on identifying and rewarding achievement, feeding project momentum towards success. End with the beginning in mind.

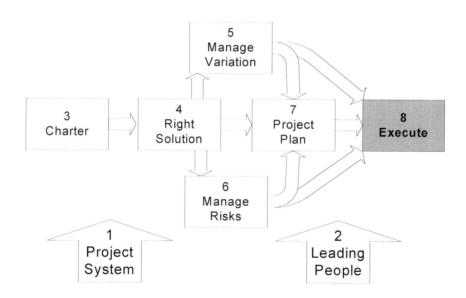

Executing Lean projects deploys the Lean principle of Pull to cause projects to flow from start to finish with minimal generation of waste. As with Lean production hand-offs from work cell to work cell, the hand-offs from one task to another are key to project flow. Ohno's relay racer analogy applies to Lean Project Management as well as it did to production. In place of the kanban card used to implement flow through visual control in manufacturing, project flow is implemented by the hand-offs from project predecessor tasks to project successor tasks. Implementing pull and enhanced flow for projects requires answering three questions, presented at the start of this chapter. The rest of the chapter focuses on how to perform buffer management: the equivalent of dealing with a line stoppage in Lean production.

LPM uses buffer management as a visual control tool during project execution to answer two or three primary questions:

1. For project, resource, and task managers: *"Which task do I work on next?"*

2. For the project leader, *"When do I take actions to accelerate the project"?*

3. For some projects, the project leader and senior management also want to know, *"How much is it going to cost?"*

The answer to the first question, addresses the task and resource manager's need to enable relay racer like task performance, avoiding bad multitasking. The answer to the second question helps the project team decide when to take action to recover buffer used up at too high a rate. The answer to the third question helps the project team decide when to take cost saving measures, or request additional budget.

The primary function of the Project Leader during execution is to help all project stakeholders achieve success by providing feedback on project success and deploying the project plan. (Plan the work, then work the plan.)

Which task do I work on next?

LPM projects require the tracking of real-time status of when tasks actually start and finish, and obtaining estimates on the remaining duration for tasks in-progress. The reason for using remaining duration rather than estimates of completion is that humans tend to over-estimate the percentage complete. When called upon to look forward and consider the work remaining to complete a task, it is possible to obtain estimates that are much more accurate. Remaining duration is also the actual number needed to project completion, and estimating it directly avoids the assumptions necessary to convert a percent complete estimate to a remaining duration estimate.

You must status your LPM schedule frequently. A general policy is:

1. Whenever a task starts,

2. Whenever a task finishes, and

3. Once a week, the day prior to the project progress meeting.

Short duration projects with short duration tasks may require status as often as once every shift. Your status duration depends mostly on the average duration of your tasks. To provide resources an accurate answer to the first question, you must have the completion of predecessor tasks accurate each time a resource is available to query the task list.

Using task priority this way enables resources to focus on one project task as a time, thereby completing it in the minimum possible time. **Tasks do not have due dates.** This helps avoid having Parkinson's Law (task durations extend to use available time) or Student Syndrome (waiting to start a task until the due date is urgent) that causes late task delivery. The ability to update remaining duration after tasks start also encourages using mean task duration estimates.

Figure 8-1 illustrates a Task Manager view into a LPM project that is underway. The tasks are color coded in the task number box on the left (not visible in the graphic) to highlight the priority of the task. Red tasks get the highest priority, as they are on a path that is causing significant project buffer use.

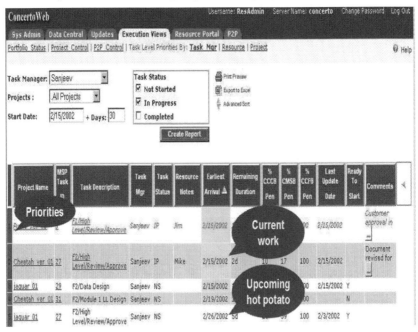

Figure 8-1: Critical chain software updates tasks using remaining duration, prioritizing tasks to be worked on. (Used by permission from Realization, Inc.)

When are you going to be done?

The amount of project buffer penetration provides the signal to take proactive action to recover buffer, while minimizing the mistake of tampering. Figure 8-2 shows the trend of buffer penetration, enabling anticipatory action and easy determination of the effectiveness of buffer recovery action. If the buffer is in the yellow (middle) region, you should develop plans to recover buffer. If the buffer penetration moves into the red (upper) region, implement the buffer recovery actions. This approach causes the project team to focus on the tasks delaying the project. Because of the green, yellow, and red colors, people often call this type of chart a fever chart. The fever chart implements the Lean manufacturing idea of visual control for projects.

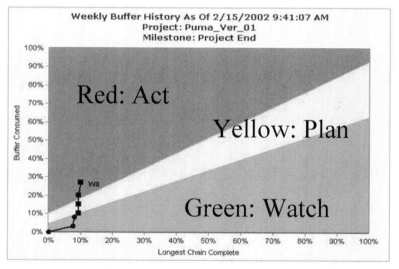

Figure 8-2: Tracking project progress with a 'fever chart' signals the project team when to take action to recover buffer.

Figure 8-3 illustrates the primary method used by LPM to track schedule performance on a portfolio of projects. The project tracking must be timely to aid the operational purposes of project management, thereby giving portfolio managers better insight to the performance of projects than many systems.

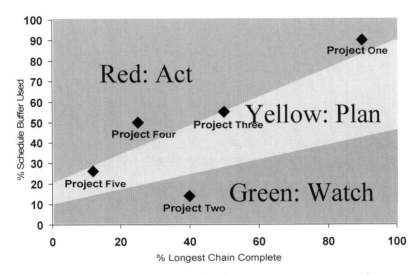

Figure 8-3: LPM simplifies viewing progress on a project portfolio, highlighting those requiring buffer recover action.

A table accompanies Figure 8-3 to provide the current projected completion date for each project, compared to the scheduled completion (i.e. when the project buffer would be 100% consumed). This directly answers the question asked.

Table 8-1: Example excerpt from status table sorts by buffer penetration and provides latest revised estimate of project completion.

#	Project Name	Due Date	Buffer Penetration (%)	Estimated Completion Date
12	Project One	2/15/05	90	4/15/05
7	Project Three	6/10/05	55	10/10/05
23	Project Four	4/15/05	50	6/12/05
13	Project Five	7/15/05	27	9/15/05

Projects that are in the green (lower region) are doing fine, and require no management attention. Projects in the yellow (middle region) should be creating buffer recovery plans. Projects in the red (upper region) should be implementing buffer recovery plans. Note that projects with buffer penetration less than 100% may still be on track to complete on time. Management should drill down for projects in the red to examine the trends and efficacy of the buffer recovery actions.

How much is it going to cost?

For some types of projects, the TOC approach clarifies that project investment cost is much less important than previously thought. For example, the impact of completing new product development projects as soon as possible to gain the first to market advantage usually far outweighs the cost to accelerate the project. However, in certain situations and for certain types of projects, cost can be important. For example, a company doing primarily fixed price projects on contract can make or lose money based on project cost.

When project cost is important, the earned value method of comparing actual cost to estimated cost becomes necessary. The reason is that actual cost is influenced by schedule. Understanding how a project is performing on cost relative to the estimate requires removing the confounding effect of schedule because a project may appear to be over or under on cost, but may actually be ahead or behind on schedule.

For this purpose, you should use a cost buffer (Leach, 2004, pps. 174-179). The cost buffer is the cost equivalent to the schedule buffers described above. There should be one cost buffer for the project. The total project estimate is the sum of the task estimates plus the cost buffer. You should estimate the cost buffer considering the cost variation of each of the project cost elements.

You can track cost buffer penetration using the same graphics presented above for schedule buffer tracking. The only difference required is to change the abscissa to represent percentage *of the task budget expended*. You can use both the single project trend version of the chart (Figure 8-2), and the multi-project point version (Figure 8-3).

You should estimate cost buffer penetration as percent of the cost buffer consumed. The earned value cost variance (CV) is the amount of cost buffer consumed. Using the cost buffer this way is an excellent example of combining conventional project management methods with LPM.

Buffer Recovery

You should formally exercise buffer recovery planning when your project time or cost buffer enters the yellow, or is trending towards the red. You should implement buffer recovery whenever your project time or cost buffer is in the red, or trending towards it. You should be sure to put the buffer recovery plan in writing, and communicate it to project stakeholders. You should also then follow-up to ensure that implementation has occurred, and that it has the desired effect.

Do not overlook simple remedies to recover buffers; e.g. making it possible for the necessary resources to focus on the correct tasks as relay racers, or authorizing overtime or extended workweeks for the resources working on the tasks in the chain causing project buffer penetration. Keep in mind that you do not have to effect buffer recovery with the task being worked: you can look down the chain for the best opportunities to recover buffer. Also, keep in mind that the currently working task may not be the cause of the buffer penetration: one of the predecessor tasks in the chain may have caused the delay, and handed it on as a hot potato to the currently working task.

A second level of buffer recovery options may involve more elegant remedies, such as reassigning resources you can better exploit the key resources, or elevating resources. You may look within the tasks for ways to accomplish them faster or cheaper. If buffer recovery options are not immediately forthcoming at this level, you can dig deeper using some of the creative tools I discussed with principle four.

Schedule and cost buffer tracking sometimes give contrary indications: you may be in the red on both cost and schedule. Some options to accelerate schedule may require additional expenditures. Some options to reduce cost may adversely affect schedule. Understanding the impacts on project benefits may help you resolve such conflicts. Table 8-2 provides some general advice.

Table 8-2: General advice when comparing cost and schedule buffer penetration indications.

		Cost Buffer	
		Red	**Green**
Schedule Buffer	**Red**	Implement no-cost or low-cost schedule acceleration and cost saving that will not affect schedule, assess additional acceleration vs. project Throughput value.	Implement schedule acceleration, including actions that increase cost.
	Green	Implement cost savings that make sense relative to project Throughput value.	Take no control action.

Sometimes you will encounter situations where the project time or cost buffer is trending upwards or remaining at a penetration level of greater than 100%, and your team is unable to come up with effective recovery alternatives, even with significant effort at applying the creative processes. In those cases, it is time to process a project change, and replan the project forward. There is little joy in leading people on a lost cause.

Fortunately, with LPM the times this happens are rare and usually caused by one of your pre-identified risk factors. In that case, stakeholder endorsement of the revised plan is usually quite easy.

Project Execution Process Management

Project Leaders must ensure execution of the project processes laid out in the project plan. The most important processes for all projects are:

- Communication,
- Quality, and
- Change control processes.

Other projects may require focused attention on additional processes, such as unit and integrated system test, issue and action resolution, safety, configuration management, or environmental control. When conflicts seem to arise between these processes and scope, schedule, or cost control, use the Evaporating Cloud to create win-win solutions.

The most important function of the Project Leader during execution is to identify and reward success. Do not forget to do so on a weekly basis, and celebrate major project milestones at least once every two or three months, so you maintain your project's positive momentum towards success!

End With the Beginning in Mind

The nature of projects is that they end. You should begin your project with the end in mind by planning on project closure from the beginning. You should end the project with the beginning in mind by bringing all of the project stakeholders back together to celebrate the achievement of their Vision.

Planning for the end of projects is serious business, not to be taken lightly. Projects sometimes get in trouble near the end by not planning for successful completion and closure of the project. Sometimes people who should have left a project with a life-long feeling of accomplishment leave disgruntled and distressed because their fate was not a part of project planning. You can prevent those undesirable outcomes by planning for project completion and closeout from the beginning.

Planning for project completion depends on the product the product the project produces. My first large projects were complex facilities, requiring extensive component and system operational testing before turnover, a system at a time, to the owner/operator. Planning and executing the test program was a major work package in the project. Performing of system readiness reviews, assuring that people, procedures, facilities and the interfaces between them were ready for the tests and then full operation were significant work packages. The planning for turnover started right after preliminary system design, and actual testing and turnover consumed the last third of the project. Later, with large IT projects, the unit, integrated system testing, and rollout of the applications were the key efforts necessary to assure project completion.

Project closure includes closing all of the project facilities, administrative closure (closing the books), and ensuring that all project stakeholders have been enabled to move on to their next venture. You should also have a great party!

Summary of the Eighth Principle

- ❑ Task execution follows the relay racer principle.
  - ○ Start as soon as input is available.
  - ○ Work 100% on one task at a time.
  - ○ Pass on the results as soon as the task is done.
- ❑ Status tasks with an estimate of the Remaining Duration (RDU) to complete.
- ❑ Use project buffer penetration to:
  - ○ Decide, "Which task do I work on next?"
  - ○ Determine when and where to take buffer recovery actions, and
  - ○ Answer, "When are you going to be done?"
- ❑ Use cost buffer penetration to answer, "How much is it going to cost?"
- ❑ Plan buffer recovery when buffers reach the yellow indication or show an adverse trend.
- ❑ Manage project processes to project success, with emphasis on project communication and change control management.

Discussion Questions:

1. Compare and contrast the methods for statusing projects you have used to the LPM methods. What are the advantages and disadvantages of each?

2. Discuss the frequency of task statusing in your projects, and how it compares to what you need for LPM.

3. List things you might do to accelerate schedule at no cost.

4. List things you might do to save cost with no schedule impact.

5. How would you do the trade-off when you are in the red regions of both the cost and schedule buffer?

6. Discuss how your project execution uses visual control.

7. Describe how your project execution implements pull.

8. Describe how your project execution responds to buffer signals (the equivalent of line stoppage in Lean manufacturing.)

References

Leach, L. (2004). *Critical Chan Project Management, Second Edition.* Boston: Artech House

Glossary

Activity The lowest level of the work breakdown structure (WBS); a packet of work that forms the basic building block of a plan or network. An activity usually requires inputs, is a process step, always creates an output, and usually has resources and duration assigned to it. I usually define activities with at least a two-word pair: verb-noun, with the verb describing the process within the activity. Interchangeable with task.

Activity network A network made up of two or more activities with a precedence relationship.

Bottleneck The constraint to Throughput in a production flow process. The limiting capacity process step.

Buffer In process inventory, time or budget allowance used to protect scheduled throughput, delivery dates, or cost estimates on a production process or project.

Buffer Management

- Weekly updating and communication of projects' buffer status by asking "how many working days to complete?" for all tasks currently in work, and projecting buffer penetration.

- Actions by Project Managers in response to the buffer report. If buffers are green, Project Managers should take no action. If yellow, they should plan how to recover time by looking down the chain from the current working task. If red, they should implement the recovery plan.

- Actions by task resources to select which task to work on next when presented with multiple tasks. Resources should work on critical chain tasks over non-critical chain tasks. If presented with multiple critical chain tasks, or multiple non-critical chain tasks, resources should work on the task with the greatest % buffer penetration.

Buffer Penetration The amount of buffer projected to be consumed comparing the current status of the project network, actual durations for completed activities, projected days to complete for working activities, and estimated (mean) duration for future activities. Sometimes called Buffer Incursion.

Capacity Buffer aka Capacity Constraint Buffer (CCB) The buffer that sequences projects. It is part of the Drum schedule. Size the capacity buffer to at least 25% of the drum resource capacity.

Cloud (EVAPORATING) See Evaporating Cloud.

Conflict Resolution Diagram (CRD) Another name for the Evaporating Cloud.

Constraint In general systems thinking, a limit to a system entity or relationship. In TOC, the process or process step that limits Throughput. In CCPM, the Critical Chain of a single project, or the Drum Resource in a multi-project environment. In project terminology, limitations placed on scheduling a task; e.g. 'Start no earlier than.

Cost Buffer The contingency or management reserve added to the sum of the project mean task estimates to create the project baseline budget. You can use the cost buffer to manage project cost. Cost buffer penetration is the cost variance from earned value: See the Project Management Institute's Project Management Body of Knowledge (PMBOK) or other project resources to understand Earned Value.

Critical Chain The longest set of dependent activities, with explicit consideration of resource availability, to achieve a project goal. The Critical Chain is NOT the same as you get from performing resource leveling on a critical path schedule. The Critical Chain defines an alternate path which completes the project earlier by resolving resource contention up front.

Critical Chain Feeding Buffer (CCFB) aka Feeding buffer A time buffer at the end of a project activity chain which feeds the critical chain.

Critical Chain Resource Buffer (CCRB) A buffer placed on the critical chain to ensure that resources are available when needed to protect the critical chain schedule. This buffer is insurance of resource availability, and does not add time to the critical chain. It takes the form of a contract with the resources that ensures their availability, whether or not you are ready to use them then, through the latest time you might need the resource. Often shortened to Resource Buffer, and sometimes called Resource Flag. Rarely used.

Critical Chain Project Management (CCPM) A complete system of effective project management integrating the Critical Chain method of project time management with the other elements of the Project Management Institute's Project Management Body of Knowledge (PMBOK^{TM})

Critical Path The longest set of dependent activities in a project, not accounting for the resource constraint. See the Project Management Institute's Project Management Body of Knowledge (PMBOK) or other project resources to understand critical path

Dependent events Events in which the output of one event influences the input to another event.

DMAIC The six sigma improvement methodology: define, measure, analyze, improve and control.

DBR Drum-Buffer-Rope method for production scheduling. The drum is the capacity of the plant constraint, and is used to set the overall throughput schedule. The buffers are in process inventories strategically located to eliminate starving the constraint due to statistical fluctuations. The rope is the information connection between the constraint and material release into the process.

Drum The bottleneck processing rate, which is used to schedule an entire plant. Also refers to the bottleneck work station. In CCPM, the resource used to stagger the start of projects. It should be the most highly used resource, and one that is not easy to elevate.

Drum Buffer: Buffer placed in the project plan immediately in front of the first use of the drum resource in a project. It's purpose is to enable project acceleration if the drum resource is available early.

Size the Drum Buffer as a feeding buffer for the preceding chain in the project. Drum buffers only exist in a multiple project environment. Drum buffers are the least important buffer, and are used infrequently.

Drum Manager In Critical Chain, the manager responsible for allocation of the drum resource. The Drum Manager creates the Drum Schedule, which is used to sequence the start of projects.

Elevate The TOC term for increasing a resource.

Evaporating Cloud: A process for conflict resolution consisting of a five entity necessity tree and processes for developing and communicating to achieve win-win solutions to any conflict. In my estimation, the Evaporating Cloud is Goldratt's highest achievement.

The action alternatives are best expressed as opposites e.g., 'Do D, don't do D." The cloud has five entities and arrows: A, the *goal*, B and C, the two *needs* that must be met by D and D', respectively. Goldratt called D and D' prerequisites; but *wants* or *initial alternatives* works better for me.

You identify the assumptions underlying the arrows to resolve the cloud. You develop injections that will invalidate the assumption, and therefore invalidate the arrow and 'dissolve' the cloud.

Exploit In TOC, getting the most out of the constraint resource, in a positive sense, directed at the goal.

Feeding Buffer See Critical Chain Feeding Buffer.

Five Focusing Steps: The five steps to deploy the Theory of Constraints:

- o IDENTIFY the constraint to the goal

- o EXPLOIT

- o SUBORDINATE

- o ELEVATE

- o Do not let INERTIA prevent you from doing it again.

Five Ss. A Lean manufacturing term referring to five words to create workplaces suited to visual control and lean production:

- o **Seri-** separate needed tools and parts

- o **Seiton-** neatly arrange tools and parts

- o **Seise-** conduct a cleanup campaign

- o **Sieketsu-** conduct the previous three at daily intervals

- o **Shisuke-** form the inner habit of performing the first four

Float In critical path, the difference in path length between the critical path and converging path. Also called slack. Float is often confused with Feeding Buffers. It is not the same. Float is an accident of the network logic, and has nothing to do with the uncertainty of the duration of the tasks in the chain. Float varies inversely with the necessary size of feeding buffers, and thus does not provide protection for uncertainty in task duration.

Goal The purpose for the existence of a system; or the single end that the system seeks to maximize. For profit making companies, the goal is to make money now and in the future. Not-for profit companies have alternative goals, usually expressible in terms of Throughput related to their purpose. Most organizations have a set of necessary conditions required to achieve the goal, usually including necessary conditions 1 and 2 (See in glossary).

Goal, The Book by Dr. Eliyahu M. Goldratt.

Inventory All of the money a system invests in things it intends to sell. In TOC, it extends beyond the conventional definition to include all the items traditionally considered as depreciable assets. For projects, there may be value in considering the work invested in projects as Inventory until the project is complete, and it begins to produce Throughput.

Lean A manufacturing philosophy to produce more with less, commonly linked to the Toyota Production System (TPS). The primary thrust of Lean manufacturing is to eliminate waste.

Mean The average of a group of data, also called the first moment of the data population. In a distribution skewed to the right, as most duration and cost estimates are, the mean is higher than the median. Mathematically, mean durations should be used on the Critical Chain, as they are the only statistic that adds linearly.

Median The middle value of a group of ordered data. The median is the '50/50' probability statistic, often confused with the mean or the mode.

Mode The most frequent value of a population.

Muda The Japanese word for waste. Lean identifies seven types of Muda:

- o **Overproduction** ahead of demand.

- o **Waiting** for the next processing step.

- o Unnecessary **transport** of material

- o **Overprocessing** of parts.

- o **Inventories** above minimum.

- o Unnecessary **movement** by employees.

- o **Defective** parts.

Need A requirement which MUST be met in order to achieve an objective or goal.

Operating Expense All of the money it costs to convert raw material into throughput.

Parkinson's Law "Work expands so as to fill the time available for its completion." Parkinson, C. (1957). *Parkinson's Law*. Cutchogue, NY; Buccaneer Books.

Pipelining The implementation of pull in a multi-project system by sequencing the start of projects to the capacity of the constraint resource (drum).

PMBOK^{TM} Project Management Body of Knowledge: The Project Management Institute's description of a complete project management system. (See www.PMI.org)

Priority The priority assigned to a project, used to determine access to the drum resource. Priority should be based on the expected project Throughput per unit of drum resource consumption. The Drum Manager uses the project priority and project schedules to level demand on the drum resource by sequencing the start of projects.

Project Charter The first document prepared for a project. It guides the team to plan the project. It includes the mission or purpose for the project (Why), the general scope, identifies the project team and stakeholders, and provides other key project parameters necessary to plan the project, such as key assumptions.

Project Execution Plan aka Project Plan, Project Management Plan, Project Work Plan: The plan for the project, describing scope, budget, schedule, the project team, project stakeholders, and project control.

Project Buffer (PB) A time buffer placed at the end of the critical chain in a project schedule to protect the overall schedule.

Pull One of the Lean principles, describing the manufacturing process of downstream processes informing upstream processes when to produce another part. In CCPM and LPM, Pipelining of projects implements Pull.

Quality Function Deployment (QFD) Akao, Y. (1990). Quality Function Deployment. Norwalk: Productivity Press, defines it two ways:

1. QFD (narrowly defined): The business or task function responsible for quality (design, manufacturing, production, etc.),

2. QFD (*broadly* defined): A combination of the business or task functions responsible for quality (design, manufacturing, production, etc.) and the quality deployment charts.

Queuing The lining up of work to be processed by a server (resource).

Relay Racer Behavior The task behavior expected of each individual working on Critical Chain projects, in which they:

- Start a task as soon as they are available and have all of the inputs,

- Work on only that one task applying 100% of their work effort, and

- Pass on the result of their work as soon as they complete it.

If presented with multiple tasks to work on, resources exhibiting Relay Runner Behavior use the Buffer report and buffer management rules to decide which task to work on next.

Resource Allocation Assigning resources to project tasks.

Resource Buffer. A buffer associated with critical chain tasks to reduce queuing delay for work on critical chain tasks. Originally conceived as a warning device to alert resources to upcoming critical chain tasks. Supplanted in most instances by filtered prioritized lists of tasks for all resources.

Resource Leveling Adjusting a project plan such that the plan demanded resources do not exceed the available resources.

Roadrunner Behavior See Relay Racer Behavior. Roadrunner was the initial metaphor suggested, but some feel that the cartoon it is based on is not the best description of the performance expectation.

Rope The information flow from the Drum (bottleneck resource) to the front of the line (material release) which controls plant Throughput.

Sequencing Scheduling the start of projects to not overload the drum resource.

SIPOC Acronym for a way of presenting a process and/or process steps:

- o Supplier
- o Input
- o Process
- o Output
- o Customer

Six Sigma A process improvement process focused on reducing variation. Six sigma refers to having less than 3.5 defects per million opportunities, considering that the mean of a statistical distribution can vary by plus or minus one sigma.

Statistical fluctuations Common cause variations in output quantity or quality.

Student Syndrome The natural tendency of many people to wait until a due date is near before applying full energy to complete the activity.

Subordinate In TOC, enabling exploiting the constraint to the goal by not allowing other things to prevent its exploitation. For example, not allowing efficiency measures to cause ineffective operation of a system to achieve the goal.

Task See activity.

Throughput The rate at which the system makes money. All of the money our customers pay us minus the raw material cost.

Theory of Constraints (TOC) A management philosophy developed by Dr. Eliyahu M. Goldratt based on the principle that complex systems exhibit inherent simplicity, i.e., even a very complex system made up of thousands of people and pieces of equipment can have any given time only a very, small number of variables – perhaps only one (know as a constraint) – that actually limits the ability to generate more of the system's goal.

Value One of the key Lean principles: the customer defined capability at the right time and place.

Value Stream All of the processes that deliver customer value.

Visual Control A Lean philosophy to simplify control for the workers with effective visual displays.

Want The effect that one believes MUST exist in order to satisfy a need, because of some set of ASSUMPTIONS.

Work Breakdown Structure (WBS) A hierarchical representation of the deliverables of a project. The starting point for project scope definition and integration of the project.

Work Package A grouping of one to around twenty-five project tasks to enable effective network planning and control during execution. A work package may have some similarity to cell in production.

Index

PMI, 6, 7, 8, 18, 37, 44, 45, 68, 70,
72, 83, 105, 107, 117, 121, 141,
145, 158, 160, 161, 163, 220
Prerequisite Tree, 220
Priority, 175, 220
list, 175, 220
project, 175, 220
task, 175, 220

Q

queue, 137

R

Relay racer, 130, 140, 199
Resource, 51, 52, 57, 58, 136, 174,
176, 181, 214, 215, 222
leveling, 51, 52, 57, 58, 136, 174,
176, 181, 214, 215, 222
loading, 51, 52, 57, 58, 136, 174,
176, 181, 214, 215, 222
Manager, 51, 52, 57, 58, 136,
174, 176, 181, 214, 215, 222
Resource Buffer, 215, 222
Responsibility, 59, 66, 115
Risk, 131, 145, 146, 147, 148, 149,
151, 153, 156-158
ident, 131, 145, 146, 147, 148,
149, 151, 153, 156, 157, 158
mitigate, 131, 145-149, 151, 153,
156-158
prevent, 131, 145, 146-149, 151,
153, 156-158
Role, 52, 55, 57

S

Schedule
buffer, 33, 134, 135, 136, 141,
147, 164, 207, 216
overrun, 33, 134, 135, 136, 141,
147, 164, 207, 216
risk, 33, 134-136, 141, 147, 164,
207, 216
variance, 33, 134-136, 141, 147,
164, 207, 216
Sequence, 112-114, 116

project, 112, 113, 114, 116
task, 112, 113, 114, 116
Six Sigma, 2
Student Syndrome, 22, 129, 136,
202, 223
Subordinate, 183, 195, 223
System, 68, 90, 92, 117, 218

T

Task, 22, 23, 42, 46, 51, 52-57, 128,
129, 131, 164, 166, 168, 169,
170, 172, 179, 181, 182, 210, 223
duration, 22, 23, 42, 46, 51-53,
55-57, 128, 129, 131, 164,
166, 168, 169, 170, 172, 179,
181, 182, 210, 223
Manager, 22, 23, 42, 46, 51-53,
55-57, 128, 129, 131, 164,
166, 168-170, 172, 179, 181,
182, 210, 223
Theory of Constraints, 2, 10, 37, 98,
117, 223
Throughput, 29, 207, 213, 214, 218,
220, 222, 223
TOC, 2, 10, 14, 24, 25, 27, 29, 31-
33, 205, 214, 216-218, 222, 223
constraint, 2, 10, 14, 24, 25, 27,
29, 31-33, 205, 214, 216-218,
222, 223
five focusing steps, 2, 10, 14, 24,
25, 27, 29, 31, 32, 33, 205,
214, 216-218, 222, 223
TRIZ, 101, 102, 116

U

Uncertainty, 120, 145

V

Variation, 119, 121, 126, 128, 133,
135, 136, 145
common, 119, 121, 126, 128,
133, 135, 136, 145
special, 119, 121, 126, 128, 133,
135, 136, 145

understanding, 119, 121, 126, 128, 133, 135, 136, 145

W

WBS, 34, 44, 59, 106-111, 113, 114-116, 163, 165, 166, 168, 169, 176, 179, 181, 188, 213, 224

Work Breakdown Structure, 34, 59, 81, 106, 117, 163, 188, 224
Work Package, 52, 107, 108, 114, 115, 116, 168